The Hockey Coaching Bible

Contents

Acknowledgments

I would like to dedicate this book to the late E.J. McGuire, who contributed chapter 13 in this collection. E.J. spent time in both college hockey and in the National Hockey League and always had time to talk hockey and make the game better. He has been missed.

While my name has a prominent place on the front cover, I need to acknowledge a few people who kept this project on track over a long period of time. First of all, Justin Klug of Human Kinetics kept the pressure on when busy authors were trying to coach their hockey teams and I was reluctant to bother them. He persevered, which led me to meet my responsibilities, and the coaches delivered.

Cynthia McEntire and Nicole Moore led the way as we approached the end of the third period, making sure final details were given proper attention.

And throughout the key editing process, Brion O'Connor was the perfect collaborator for this project: a part-time hockey coach whose full-time job is freelance writer and editor. The project could not have had a better person in his role as he was as comfortable at his keyboard as he was on the ice.

And of course, thanks to all the contributing authors who share a common passion for the game and the ability to communicate so that others may learn and add to our beloved ice hockey culture.

Introduction

On February 1, 1896, Johns Hopkins University hosted Yale University in the first ice hockey game played between two American college teams. The game that day—a 2-2 tie—took place in a Baltimore arena that was destroyed by fire not long after that season, contributing to the end of the Johns Hopkins program (the university returned as a club team after a 90-year hiatus). Yale hockey lived on and prospered, and the Bulldogs eventually won their first national championship in the sport in 2013.

The hockey on display that day was a distant cousin of today's game, not only in the skill and style displayed on the ice, but also in the entire presentation of the event. College hockey today is a thrilling game played in state-of-the-art arenas, its pageantry captured on regional and national television, and its star players moving on to the National Hockey League (NHL) in record numbers.

During the 2013-2014 season, a record 305 former college players made it to NHL rosters, making up 31 percent of the league. With a growing number of former collegians filling general manager and other executive positions, it is not surprising that NCAA hockey has become the fastest-growing development path to the NHL.

ICE HOCKEY IN THE NCAA

Part of the growth of college hockey stems from the institutional growth of the National Collegiate Athletic Association (NCAA) and, perhaps more significantly, from the growth of sport-specific organizations such as the American Hockey Coaches Association (AHCA) and the many hockey conferences that administer the sport daily.

The NCAA interacts with college hockey in three significant ways: through the administration of the national championship, through the work of the NCAA Men's and Women's Ice Hockey Rules Committee, and through enforcement of the many bylaws that govern intercollegiate athletics.

The NCAA Division I Men's Ice Hockey Championship, culminating in the annual Frozen Four each spring, has become one of the most successful of the NCAA's many postseason tournaments. The event had its origin in 1948 in Colorado Springs, where it resided for the first 10 years of its existence. For the next few decades, the championships remained somewhat modest, often played on college campuses.

All that changed in the 1990s when large urban arenas began bidding for the event, reflecting the growth in the popularity of college hockey. Since then, the Frozen Four has played to sold-out crowds in NHL buildings, not only frequenting the college hockey hotbeds of Boston, St. Paul, and Detroit, but also finding welcoming crowds in St. Louis, Anaheim, and Tampa.

The NCAA Rules Committee has brought together men and women from coaching and administrative backgrounds to ensure that the playing rules keep pace with positive changes in the game while, at the same time, focusing on the traditional issues of safety and fair play.

The third leg of NCAA interaction with college hockey has been less kind to the sport. The NCAA bylaws are not created with individual sports in mind, so the interests of the ice hockey community aren't always taken into consideration. As the excesses of other sports, most notably basketball and football, have led to oversized rule manuals, ice hockey has had to fall in line with all other sports, despite being unique in two significant ways.

First, just shy of 30 percent of men's Division I ice hockey programs reside at schools that are NCAA Division II or Division III institutions. College hockey was born in small towns in northern climates. And while that profile has changed, it remains a big part of what the college hockey culture is. The NCAA once allowed schools to play up in one male sport and one female sport. As a result, we have many Division III schools—such as Colorado College, Rensselaer Polytechnic Institute, Clarkson University, and others—playing hockey at the Division I level.

In fact, there are more Division II and Division III schools who have opted to play up in ice hockey than have opted to play Division I in all of the other NCAA Division I sports combined. The NCAA has done away with this option, closing the door on a number of other institutions that would have considered a move to Division I ice hockey.

The other unique factor that affects NCAA men's Division I ice hockey is the existence of junior hockey in Canada, where the top level competes for young hockey players and is deemed a professional league by the NCAA. In recent years, these junior leagues have become more aggressive in their recruitment of players, and in 2014 some 120 Americans opted to play in Canada rather than attend a U.S. college.

Where NCAA hockey coaches must follow the NCAA rules on amateurism and recruiting, Canada's junior teams don't have the same restrictions. Unfortunately, today's college hockey coaches, along with their school and conference administrators, haven't been able to fashion rules and policies that would help create a level playing field when dealing with representatives of junior hockey.

AMERICAN HOCKEY COACHES ASSOCIATION

These obstacles would be even more challenging if not for the efforts of a number of hockey-specific organizations. The American Hockey Coaches Association (AHCA) was formed in 1947 to provide amateur coaches a structure within which they could exchange ideas, modify rules, and recognize accomplishments.

The AHCA began with informal meetings in Boston or at the NCAA tournament with perhaps 50 or 60 coaches getting together in a hotel to discuss the issues of the day. Today, the AHCA has more than 1,400 members, and an annual convention in Naples, Florida that attracts close to 700 people each spring.

As in those early years, the coaches share their thoughts on such things as playing rules and recruiting practices, while still taking time to honor unique contributions to the game through the selection of All-American awards for current players and memorialized awards for retired coaches and other contributors.

Outside speakers are brought in to accompany active AHCA members in a series of talks and drill sessions, just as they have done for the past seven decades. It was through the AHCA that most of the authors in this book were contacted and asked to contribute their chapters.

DIVISION I CONFERENCES

Other sport-specific organizations include the hockey conferences that assume administrative responsibility for college hockey. Up until the Big Ten formed a hockey conference in 2013, NCAA Division I hockey was administered by single-sport conferences: the Atlantic Hockey Association, the Central Collegiate Hockey Association, the Eastern College Athletic Conference, the Hockey East Association, and the Western Collegiate Hockey Association. The commissioners of these respective conferences began meeting regularly and harmoniously in the late 1980s, changing what had been a landscape of east versus west in many ways. As more structured meetings took place, the commissioners began to realize that despite the inherent competitive nature of the institutions, the sport would not advance if the parties put self-interest and regional affiliations ahead of growing the game.

So, the group followed years of loosely organized meetings at the NCAA tournament or, perhaps, at the AHCA convention, and created the Hockey Commissioners Association (HCA) in 2003. Two goals of the HCA were to increase the exposure of college hockey on television and to seek funding from the NHL to assist in the advancement and growth of college hockey in the United States.

The television portion came to fruition through a combination of factors, most notably the growth in sports networks starting in the 1990s and the sharp rise of college talent in the NHL. The funding goal was reached in 2009 when the NHL committed $8 million annually to USA Hockey to grow the game in the United States, and the NHL encouraged USA Hockey to assign some of that revenue to the college hockey community.

USA Hockey, negotiating with the HCA, did indeed earmark significant funds for college hockey, which led to the creation of College Hockey, Inc. (CHI), the recruiting and marketing arm of NCAA Division I men's ice hockey. In addition to serving on the front lines in the battle with Canadian junior hockey, CHI has been working to grow the college game in a literal sense by encouraging new programs, many in new nontraditional locales. The first victory in this campaign was the announcement in November of 2014 by Arizona State University that it was elevating its club program to varsity status in 2015.

SHARING KNOWLEDGE

Many coaches who have been around the game for a number of decades likely have a weathered edition of Eddie Jeremiah's *Ice Hockey* or Lloyd Percival's *The Hockey Handbook*. For generations, these were the go-to tomes for solid hockey instruction.

Later, these sources were replaced by the terrific work produced by USA Hockey, either through in-person clinics or online modules, bringing common and current instruction to everyone from the local youth coach to the college hockey veteran. Alongside the teachings emanating from this national governing body, a variety of coaches have produced local works, in print or on DVD.

In this collection of instructional and educational essays, an impressive cross-section of hockey coaches share what their hockey lives have taught them. Most of the authors remain active in college hockey today. Some have spent time in professional hockey, either before or after enjoying a college hockey experience.

The topics covered range from the philosophical to the technical. Here, in order of presentation, is a summary of each author's topic and background.

Chapter 1: "Keeping a balance" is the mantra of Bill Cleary, the former Harvard University player, coach, and athletic director. Cleary, who set a single-season scoring record in the mid-1950s that still stands, won Olympic silver (1956) and gold (1960) as a player and an NCAA title as a coach (1989). As competitive as Cleary was by nature, he always kept things fun.

Chapter 2: Tom Anastos of Michigan State is another hockey player who went back to his alma mater as head coach. In between, Anastos served as commissioner of the Central Collegiate Hockey Association. He is also the parent of a Division I women's hockey player. In all of his roles, he has lived the values he offers in his chapter on coaching with integrity.

Chapter 3: When Guy Gadowsky left Princeton University to oversee the Penn State club team's elevation to varsity status, he had to deal with more than Xs and Os on the ice. Part of his challenge is addressed in Communicating a Team Mission. Gadowsky, a native of Edmonton, played at Colorado College and launched his head-coaching career at Alaska.

Chapter 4: Mike Schafer began his 20th season as head coach of Cornell University in the fall of 2014, and he is closing in on 400 career wins. Like so many authors in this book, Schafer attended the school at which he coaches. A two-time captain at Cornell and a member of the class of 1986, Schafer has been a leader as both player and coach. His accomplishments make him more than qualified to address the topic of acting as a professional.

Chapter 5: In his many years coaching youth hockey, Marty Palma, the head coach at the Community College of Allegheny County, has discovered creative ways to involve parents, fans, and the community at large.

Chapter 6: Although most of the authors come from college hockey, most of our readers are likely to be involved at lower levels. So we turned to Hal Tearse, a 40-year veteran of youth, high school, and college experiences in Minnesota, to pen the chapter on building a high school program. In addition to his coaching, Tearse has authored numerous articles and videos addressing on-ice and off-ice issues for a variety of Minnesota organizations.

Chapter 7: University of Connecticut head coach Mike Cavanaugh shares his thoughts on planning and conducting productive practices. Before landing his first head-coaching job in 2013, Cavanaugh played for Terry Meagher at Bowdoin College for four years and worked beside Jerry York for 19 years at Bowling Green and Boston College. Cavanaugh's years as an assistant were recognized by the AHCA when he received the Terry Flanagan Award for his career body of work in 2013.

Chapter 8: This chapter begins a string of three chapters addressing position-specific skills. Legendary Boston University coach Jack Parker addresses skills for defensemen, something he enjoyed in abundance during his 40 years and 897 wins with the Terriers. Among those successes were NCAA titles in 1978, 1995, and 2009. Parker played and captained BU as an undergraduate.

Chapter 9: Another NCAA champion, Rick Comley, contributes the chapter Skills for Forwards. Comley, who played at Lake Superior State University, started his head-coaching career at LSSU before moving on to Northern Michigan and Michigan State. He won NCAA titles at NMU (1991) and MSU (2007). In his 38-year head-coaching career, Comley won 783 games.

Chapter 10: Editor Joe Bertagna contributed the chapter Skills for Goaltenders. The information passed along here was mined in a coaching career that is now in its fifth decade. In addition to coaching goalies of all ages in summer camps and winter clinics in the Boston area, Bertagna spent six seasons as goalie coach with the Boston Bruins (1985-1991) and also enjoyed that role with the 1994 U.S. Olympic team. The highlight of his Harvard playing days just might have been playing a goalie in the movie *Love Story*.

Chapter 11: The book concludes with six chapters devoted to team play and systems. Launching these is a look at defensive zone play contributed by Mark Dennehy, head coach at Merrimack College. A former Boston College player, Dennehy had a brief stint as head coach at Fairfield University before toiling as an assistant coach with Don "Toot" Cahoon at Princeton and the University of Massachusetts. He has revitalized the Merrimack Warrior hockey program.

Chapter 12: For our consideration of neutral zone play, we turned to a veteran of both college and international hockey. Ben Smith played at Harvard; assisted legendary coaches Tim Taylor and Jack Parker at Yale and Boston University, respectively; and then launched a successful head-coaching career with Dartmouth, Northeastern, and the U.S. women's Olympic team. In his latter role, Smith led the USA to gold (1998), silver (2002), and bronze (2006) in three Olympic Games.

Chapter 13: One of the most generous authors in our lineup was the late E.J. McGuire, who passed away shortly after contributing his chapter, Offensive Zone Attack. McGuire, who was working as the NHL's director of central scouting at the time of his death, moved into scouting after 12 seasons as an NHL assistant with the Philadelphia Flyers and Chicago Blackhawks. He had previously worked at the college level and was known as a friend to all, ready to offer his insights and assistance wherever needed.

Chapter 14: Another of our authors who moved from the college ranks to the NHL is George Gwozdecky, who has contributed Special Teams and Situations. Gwozdecky, who played at the University of Wisconsin, has experienced success as both a player and coach, winning NCAA titles as a Badger in 1977 and then back to back as head coach with Denver (2004 and 2005). Now an assistant coach with Tampa Bay of the NHL, he also served as head coach at Miami University.

Contributing to chapter 14 is Michael Zucker, co-founder of Bench Metrics LLC, a software company in hockey analytics. He has helped coach 39 NHL draft picks and has been coaching hockey since 1997.

Chapter 15: One of the bright young coaches in the game today is Nate Leaman of Providence College. Leaman, whose topic is scouting opponents, took Union College to its first ECAC championship before moving on to guide Providence to its highest finish in Hockey East in nearly a decade. His work at Union is also credited with laying the foundation for the school's 2014 NCAA championship. In 2015 he coached Providence College to the NCAA Championship.

Chapter 16: We finish with International Play by University of Wisconsin head coach Mike Eaves. Eaves is the sixth coach in our lineup to have played and coached at the same university. A two-time All-American and a member of the Badgers' 1977 NCAA championship team, Eaves played for eight NHL seasons. He then launched a career that included assignments in the NHL and with USA Hockey before returning to Madison in 2002. He led the Badgers to the school's sixth NCAA title in 2006 and has seen both of his sons, Ben and Patrick, enjoy college and professional careers.

Keeping a Balance

Bill Cleary

Hockey provides many wonderful experiences for many competitors. For all of those players who have competed, these moments have been a key part of their life experiences, providing a stepping stone to future endeavors, whether in or out of the game.

Having been involved for more than 50 years as a student, player, coach, referee, and athletic director, I've seen many changes. Change is important, and in many cases, change means progress. However, not all changes have been good for the general welfare of the players, especially student-athletes. Many changes have taken us far afield from our mission.

The growing and consistent pressure on coaches at all levels to win often makes it easy for them to neglect why we are in this business. For college coaches, our job is to provide appropriate athletic opportunities for student-athletes, always remembering we do so as educators first and foremost. In looking at recent trends, there is an emerging concern that we are straying from this stated purpose. It is natural for coaches to strive to get a competitive advantage, so long as it is done within the true spirit of intercollegiate athletics. Putting winning first can lead to some dangerous excesses.

Three areas concern me about today's intercollegiate ice hockey climate: the style of play, recruiting practices, and the role of fun in the total experience.

STYLE OF PLAY

College hockey should be a skillful sport, one that when played properly is a thing of beauty. Presently, skill and finesse appear to be lost arts. Too often, today's game resembles football on ice. Starting with youth hockey, the game frequently becomes a scrum along the boards and in the corners. Rarely do we see wide-open games with players showcasing the skills of stickhandling, passing, and shooting. Body checking by hitting the opponent with a hip or shoulder in the middle of the ice was once an art. Today, body checking means running the opponent into the boards, frequently from behind, which by its very nature puts a player at serious risk of injury.

Many people, notably the members of the NCAA Ice Hockey Rules Committee, are tinkering with various aspects of the game to improve its appeal to fans and players alike. An obvious place to start is proper enforcement of existing rules. If coaches and officials ignore the rules or apply their own loose interpretations, they in effect reward those who break the rules.

Specific rules prohibit infractions such as holding, hooking, interference, charging, board checking, and the like. If not called, these penalties might as well be eliminated from the rulebook. On the other hand, if NCAA officials, from conference offices to the referees on the ice, enforce the rulebook, penalties will be called more consistently, players and coaches will adjust, and fans will see the game that once prospered. In the end, skill will return to the game and skilled players will flourish. The NCAA recently began an effort to make the words in the rulebook mean something, and the public response was favorable. Even officials with the pro leagues are starting to call the game more tightly.

Another factor has been the recent trend toward older players in the college game, partly the result of student-athletes pursuing hockey experiences in junior leagues after high school or prep school. In some cases, colleges have encouraged this trend. In others, the family has made a number of decisions in search of the perfect hockey path. Whatever the reason, the net effect has resulted in 21-year-old freshmen being commonplace.

This phenomenon has led some observers to note that college coaches inherit players well versed in circumventing the spirit of the rulebook. Although some of today's players arrive on campus well versed in clutching, grabbing, and taking the occasional dive, it remains the responsibility of college coaches to break them of these habits. It is never enough to say, "We don't teach that." If the players are doing it, whether you taught them or not, it is your job as a coach to put an end to that behavior. The coaches are ultimately responsible for what their players bring to the game.

RECRUITING PRACTICES

The second area of concern in today's game is recruiting, which has become a nightmare for coaches and recruits alike. We are collectively pressuring students to commit to colleges too early in their high school careers. I say collectively because some athletes, their parents, and the more aggressive coaches all contribute to this growing phenomenon. In reality, this is not a practice that benefits coaches or students.

At top levels of college hockey it has become nearly impossible to come to school directly from a high school experience without taking a year or two to pursue a hockey-only stint at the junior level. This is part of the professionalization of our sport. Postsecondary school decisions are often based solely on hockey and not academics or other factors.

Two of the more hotly debated issues among college coaches in recent years are verbal commitments and the lack of a recruiting calendar for coaches. Young student-athletes are making verbal commitments to colleges as early as their freshman and sophomore years of high school, and there have been high-profile athletes that commit as early as eighth grade. College coaches expect these commitments to be honored and most are. But less scrupulous coaches find it difficult not to butt in and recruit promising young players who have already made verbal commitments. These situations compromise the integrity that should exist among the college coaching community.

Often, the source of the problem isn't the college coach but the athlete's family. Parents start to think their child can do better at a different school and make it known through intermediaries that their child's commitment might not be ironclad if a better offer came along. Then coaches can get caught in the crossfire. A coach's best approach is to be up front with the student, his or her family, and fellow coaches. But the process is certainly more aggressive than ever.

This issue highlights the need for an established recruiting calendar, a mutually agreed upon schedule that would limit when active evaluation of and contact with recruits can take place. Other sports have such a process, but ice hockey has been slow to embrace the structure such a calendar would provide. Assistant hockey coaches are challenged to have a healthy family life of their own when they have to respond to the pressures of keeping up with the competition. No one wants to take themselves out of the race for top players for fear that the competition will get an advantage. The time has come for such a calendar and reasonable restrictions.

Some observers have suggested that key showcase events must also be accounted for. Reputable events will move to dates that the timeline allows, while others will fall by the wayside. That might just be another benefit of such a structured calendar.

THE ROLE OF FUN

My last concern is this: Are we taking the fun out of the game? I often ask this question about the college game, with which I am most familiar. College sports have become a big business. The demands on coaches and players have increased a hundredfold over the last decade or so. Colleges have built spectacular state-of-the-art facilities, and college administrators expect those facilities to be filled every night.

These arenas and stadiums offer unmatched amenities for participants and spectators alike. But they come with expectations that add to the pressures already weighing on today's coaches. The benefits are greater, but so are the stakes. More than ever, coaches understand they must be successful to keep their jobs. This can affect how programs are run and where fun fits in on a priority scale.

Practices have become more intense and are held for longer periods of time. There is a tendency to overcoach in all sports, which encourages the athletes to respond like robots. We have, to a certain degree, taken away the spontaneity of playing the game.

During the latter half of my coaching career, I came to the conclusion that no student would sit through a two- or three-hour class without nodding off or becoming bored. Why should it be any different for a sports class? It was then that I cut my practice time in half and instituted one fun day of practice each week, which in turn gave my athletes extra time for their schoolwork. It is more important for students to feel good about coming to practice and know they have time to do other things academically or socially. Mental fatigue can be the bane of any player or coach. Given the grind of a lengthy season, it's critical that students feel fresh and alert. You should be able to accomplish all you need to do in a high-tempo 90-minute practice.

It's too easy for coaches to say that since the pressures are greater, more must be asked of the athletes. I disagree. The pressure is only a problem if you want to make it a problem or allow it to be a problem. Keep practices brief, light, and up tempo, and you will get a better response from your players, which will result in more success for your program.

Finally, there is an undeniable relationship between fun and the goals that students and their families establish. College sport has become a breeding ground for the professional ranks, but the reality is that only a select few make it to the big time. The playing seasons have become longer, and out-of-season training is just as demanding. Students are no longer able to play a second sport and often are prevented from simply enjoying the other benefits of campus life.

This isn't just the fault of the schools that sponsor the sport. Many parents are part of the problem, starting with the decisions made when the hockey player is just a youngster. Kids are moved from program to program, commitments are made and broken, all in the pursuit of a perfect hockey situation. Somewhere along the line, and fairly early, the potential elite player thinks less about having fun and more about getting the prize, which could be an elite youth team, a prep school slot, a college scholarship, or a pro contract. Unfortunately, when the fun element is ignored early, the youngster often abandons the sport before the family's goals are realized.

CONCLUSION

All this leads to the obvious question: What is the purpose of collegiate hockey? Is it primarily to further the student's hockey career or to develop a more complete individual, who may or may not have a potential postgraduate playing career as an extra benefit?

Sport should not be just about winning and losing. It should be about people, competition, and performing under pressure as a group. It reveals a great deal about what people are made of and how much respect they have for others and themselves. It teaches how to accept the good and the bad. It is learning to help others, follow rules, and become better citizens. It is about setting goals, learning skills and systems, and yes, also competing to win.

2

Coaching With Integrity

Tom Anastos

It is not unusual to come across a news story or a magazine article lamenting the lack of civility and sportsmanship in the arenas where athletic events take place. Bad behavior seems to surround us, whether in youth sports or in the more elite amateur and professional ranks.

As a parent and a coach, I've witnessed examples of poor sportsmanship and questionable ethics from time to time. But, as is often the case, those who violate the spirit of good competition often get an inordinate amount of the spotlight at the expense of the vast majority of practitioners who possess a strong sense of right and wrong and rarely allow that mindset to be compromised by a desire to win.

Coaches are, at the most basic level, teachers. Their responsibilities go beyond teaching strategies to succeed in the specific sport or discipline they've chosen. Coaches, particularly those who coach at academic institutions, have a responsibility to teach life lessons to their players through the games they play.

Let's look at a number of common situations that can crop up in the course of a hockey season.

BEFORE ATHLETES ARRIVE

As a college coach, my interaction with student-athletes starts long before they step on campus. The recruiting process makes the coach a salesman, and for many of us, it's not our favorite part of the job. But the process is tempered by the fact that we believe in what we are selling, and if we pursue the right athletes, we can speak with sincerity when we suggest that they should consider our institutions. This process gives a future player a glimpse at what the coach and the program stand for.

We've all heard stories of coaches who, when speaking with a highly sought after recruit, fall into the trap of making specific promises. This probably doesn't happen as often as thought, particularly if you rule out the percentage of parents who hear what they want to hear and relay stories that are just a little self-serving and a tad inaccurate.

But, yes, coaches have promised that the young skater will not only take a regular shift but likely be on the power play, kill penalties, and certainly be a captain his senior year. And maybe the coach actually believes this is likely if the athlete shows up on campus. The problem is we don't know all of that in advance.

I want to be direct with recruits. If I think he can do all those things, I'll tell him those are a possibility. The full scholarship is a financial benefit to the family, but it doesn't earn the athlete a minute of playing time. Those who are not scholarship players have the same chance. If we are recruiting the athlete, we tell him we think he will have a strong impact on our team. Although I might not say that I have identified a recruit as a PP player, I also wouldn't say anything that closes the door on that possibility.

I tell him where I think he fits on our roster, both in his first year and over a matter of time. We tell players that very candidly. Often, I refer to that conversation with players a year or two into their careers with us.

I'll ask them if we have delivered what we promised, so I can make sure I am staying on target. In the end, I'd rather lose a prospect by telling him what I really believe is the truth than try to tiptoe around issues that I'll have to deal with in the future.

Another temptation in the recruiting process that can sometimes tarnish a coach and his reputation is making a negative comment about a competing school. We don't talk about other programs. This mirrors a personal philosophy I've embraced in my other business ventures over the years. We might reference a generic campus or other league, but even those aren't painted in a negative light. We want the recruit to hear all about what we offer on our campus and in our conference. This isn't just the right thing to do. It is also a turnoff to most people when a coach starts to be critical of the competition. The idea of focusing on your own business will come up later in a different context.

In today's climate, prospective student-athletes are making decisions earlier in the college process, and the verbal commitment is a hot topic. For example, an athlete as young as 14 or 15 and his family make a commitment to a school that is nonbinding until the student-athlete signs a National Letter of Intent. Stories abound of coaches from other schools contacting these athletes, perhaps influencing them to change their decision. Families waver. Sometimes schools waver. It can get very contentious.

When people stick to the written rule and honor both the actual rule and the spirit of the rule, there are relatively few problems. When this dynamic hinges on a gentlemen's agreement made outside the proper rules, there is frequently a breakdown of order.

We all know, or should know, the rules that apply to these situations. We also know how we would like to be treated. Know the rules, follow them, and communicate honestly and openly with people. It should be as simple as that.

RESPECT FOR RULES AND OFFICIALS

Another area that tests the integrity of coaches, players, and fans is the relationship we have with the rules of the game and those who are there to enforce the rules. As a coach, it is my responsibility to make sure the players know the rules and the consequences for breaking them. At the college level, we have NCAA-established on-ice and off-ice rules, conference rules, and team rules. Respecting rules is a priority that needs to be established early.

One area in which our culture has slipped a little is in respect for officials. How we approach officials and how we react when certain circumstances come up are things I have to anticipate and teach as part of our own team culture.

We have had on-ice situations in which officials have made egregious errors. My players will be affected by how I react in these situations. Having served as a conference commissioner, I am able to understand both sides in these situations. Sure, it's frustrating. I know that the players will take a cue from how I respond. So I want to set an example as to how we—all of us—will react when, quite clearly, we have been victimized by an incorrect call or a rule interpretation.

One approach I've taken is to emphasize that we, as a team, have to get good enough to play through bad breaks or calls that might be incorrect. We take responsibility for how things go. The focus stays on our team and those things we can control. Educated people will know when we have been the victims of something that might not have gone right. You don't need a public show to make you look better.

At the same time, there needs to be a balance. Players want to know that you will stand up for them. You can take steps privately to support your team when you feel victimized. But it does no good to make a public scene with the official in front of the team or, as sometimes happens, with the media in a postgame press conference.

Former University of Vermont head coach Mike Gilligan earned the respect of his peers when, during an NCAA Frozen Four semifinal, his fast-skating team was victimized first by sloppy ice conditions due to a broken pipe below the ice surface and second by a goal in overtime that was due, in part, to an illegal hand pass that was missed by the officials. When asked about the ice, Gilligan noted that both teams had to play under the same conditions, offered up no excuses, and gave praise to the winning team. He made no comments about the factors that led to the winning goal.

I've had some experience with poor ice conditions, once when I was a commissioner and our conference hosted an indoor Frozen Four at Detroit's Ford Field, and once when our team played outside at Comerica Park. In both instances, the ice was not up to normal expectations. I found that all the coaches did a good job acknowledging the conditions but refused to use it as an excuse.

In these instances, when players are asked, I tell them that I don't expect them to lie or make up a story. They can tell the truth about the conditions but should always acknowledge the basic point that those conditions were the same for all participants and not to use them as an excuse.

One additional angle to the participant–official relationship is that I've had officials come to me some time after an incident and acknowledge that they had reviewed a tape and seen they made a mistake. Likewise, I have gone into the locker room between periods, looked at video, and realized what I thought I saw in real time was not the case. In that instance, I made a point to come out at the start of the next period and admit I was wrong to the officials.

Isn't this the way we want people to live their lives? Taking responsibility for their actions? These are teaching moments that coaches need to capitalize on.

DOING WHAT'S RIGHT

Some time ago, we played a home game against our biggest rival. We didn't play particularly well, but we were still in the game late in the third. As the clock wound down, the other team put the game away with a shorthanded goal. Shortly thereafter, one of our seniors took a face-off at our offensive blue line. All of a sudden, our senior runs a player. It looked ridiculous and was completely out of character. It just came out of nowhere. He clearly, and quite suddenly, lost his cool.

The officials assessed a minor penalty, keeping him in the game. As the official came by our bench, I told him, "I am sending him off the ice. Assess whatever you want but he's done. I am taking him out of the game." It's easy to let the official stand in for you in your responsibility to enforce rules and expectations. But what about those situations the official doesn't see but you do?

We all see our players get away with behavior that is not representative of the team's values. And there is a wide spectrum of such behaviors. Maybe it's interference off a face-off that gives your team an edge. This might fall under gamesmanship. But what about the player who embellishes a situation and earns you a power play? When does gamesmanship cross the line into cheating? What about the slash behind the play? Now we move into dirty or dangerous play. What about a secondhand report that comes back to you that a player used a racial epithet?

Integrity is not a part-time thing. You have it all the time or you don't. In our culture, we should address situations honestly and take responsibility. At the same time, we need to assess the proper penalty for the specific violation.

We had a freshman who did something that wasn't seen by the referee. When he came off the ice, I confronted him: "If that's the way you are going to play, you will be in the stands. We want you to play tough. But dirty stuff and retaliatory stuff is not how we play. These acts are unacceptable." He didn't get to play much the rest of the game, and he knew why. I didn't immediately take him out of the game, but if his bad behavior continued,

I was prepared to take stronger steps. I wouldn't play him late in games when he couldn't control his emotions. The severity of the penalty would progress if the lack of discipline continued.

We have done the same with players who dive. They are told it is not how we play, and that it is an embarrassment to the player and the team.

As for very dangerous play or the example of the racial slur, there can't be any tolerance. You look at every situation on an individual basis, but I can't think of one situation in which this would be acceptable. Regular game, championship night, ordinary practice, it doesn't matter. Some things are just wrong, and no one gets a pass. The challenge is to make these decisions during the heat of the action when it actually happens and something is on the line.

CONCLUSION

In today's culture, winning is held in high esteem. In fact, in some circumstances, only the winning of a championship constitutes success to some participants. In the world of college athletics, what we try to do on the ice is consistent with the goals of our institution in general. We teach the values inherent in preparation, teamwork, and competition. But if we compromise sportsmanship and integrity in order to win games and trophies, we know we've failed in a greater sense.

Although we believe our student-athletes arrive on campus with a sense of right and wrong instilled in them by their families and perhaps their previous coaches, it is our job to articulate to our players and staff what we expect from them and what our team culture allows. Respect for rules must be established early. Exactly what those rules are and the consequences of breaking them must be communicated clearly. And when inappropriate behavior is exhibited, you must act decisively and with consistency.

Even before those moments, the coach and figurehead must set the example for others to follow, not for show but because it is the right way to behave and is consistent with what your program stands for. Doing so early and often makes that the norm for your program, and it makes it clear to all how they should fashion their way of conducting business.

3

Communicating a Team Mission

Guy Gadowsky

Before discussing how to communicate a team mission, I want to briefly cover coaching in general, including coaching philosophy. There is no one way to coach, not one system that is the best, and not one philosophy that is superior to any other. Many coaches have reached hockey's pinnacle—Stanley Cup champions—by employing very different systems, philosophies, and methods of motivating and communicating with their teams.

I've been extremely fortunate to play for and coach under some exceptional coaches. Early in my coaching career, I would try to copy what they did in many aspects. Before long, I realized that no matter how much I studied how they operated, if it just wasn't me, it wouldn't work. I came to realize that knowing the technique or system isn't necessarily what's important. What is imperative is that you know yourself and what works best for you. The only way to figure that out is to be yourself and communicate in a manner that is consistent with your own personality and coaching style.

In this chapter, I'll offer suggestions about self-evaluation, team building, mission statements, and effective team communication. I'll discuss some of the influences I've had that have encouraged me to try different ideas. I hope some of these suggestions will help you discover communication techniques that work well for you.

Courtesy of Steve Manuel.

CRYSTALLIZING YOUR VISION

Coaches can learn a great deal by studying how successful organizations outside of sport operate. Team building, goal setting, and communicating are just a few examples of how sports teams can emulate techniques from the military or the corporate world to benefit their own programs. Most coaches have read books on these subjects to help develop leadership skills. But by far, I've learned the most about team building and communication from the coaches I've been fortunate enough to play for or coach with. I don't know if they developed their techniques from emulating other coaches, by reading books, or simply by trial and error, but I can certainly see many of their successful techniques in the leadership books that I've read.

Similar to what you might find in corporate business journals, the first step to effectively communicating a team mission is to develop a very clear picture of the desired end product. I believe the best way to achieve this goal is through honest self-evaluation. This makes perfect sense—the better you understand what you do well and what you need to improve, the easier it is to be clear about your goals and what you want to communicate. The head coach should have a clear vision of what the end product should look like. Steven Covey, author of *The 7 Habits of Highly Successful People*, recommends starting with the end in mind. This might seem like an easy process, but it takes time and a lot of self-reflection to properly achieve this. Once you're confident with your vision, it is vital to solicit input from the entire staff to come up with the best plan to achieve that vision. Without question, the best solutions we've developed to improve the teams I've coached have come from other staff members.

You can crystallize your vision through staff retreats. This might be one of the most important things you can do as a staff to improve your program. Asking for feedback from players and staff members is sometimes uncomfortable, but if the information you gather is honest and has the program's best interests at heart, it will be valuable. In my case, the process of program evaluation came as a product of necessity. I had very little experience in college hockey when I arrived at the University of Alaska–Fairbanks straight from the West Coast Hockey League. Other than as a player, I really had no knowledge of the inner workings of a college hockey program. At the end of my first season, I needed to evaluate all aspects of the program, as much for my own education as for gathering information to prepare a plan to improve.

When taken seriously, a program evaluation should benefit the entire staff. If you are as inexperienced as I was, you'll have a lot of ground to cover, and this process can certainly take considerable time. But eventually you'll become more efficient and gather more information in a shorter time. Because of the length of our first program evaluation, one of our coaches, Kirk Patton, unaffectionately referred to the process as the Geneva Conventions, and that moniker has stuck ever since. We are now into double digits with our annual Geneva Convention, and I learn more and more from them every year. Examples of the categories of our evaluations are shown in the sidebar.

When you've completed this process, you should have a clear vision of what you want your program to look like and an honest evaluation of your current program. You can now create an internal plan for improvement.

Evaluation Categories

Systems

Philosophies

Statistics

- Team (goals against, goals scored, power-play and penalty-kill percentages, and so on)
- Individual

Personnel

- Attitude
- Performance
- Leaders
- Followers

Practices

- Times
- Length
- Positives
- Negatives

Road trips

Fund-raising

Alumni relations

Locker room environment

Academic commitment

Academic performance

INSPIRING THE BUY-IN

Once you have all your staff members on the same page, the next step is to get the team to buy into those expectations. This sounds simple, but it's easier said than done and the essence of what this chapter should address.

There are many different ways to achieve a unified team plan. One common method is to develop a shared mission or vision statement. Collaboration increases commitment, ownership, and mutual accountability. This technique is often used with sports teams and in the military, organizations, and businesses, big and small. You can find many definitions of a mission statement in different leadership or team-building publications. According to Penn State University sports psychologist Dave Yukelson, "The essence of a mission statement is to create a team identity and unity of purpose. In essence, 'This is who we are, this is what we are all about.'"

Again, to effectively create a mission or vision statement for your team or program, you need to gather input from the group. You can't expect a high level of buy-in if the individuals don't feel ownership in the vision. Creating an environment in which all players feel comfortable voicing their opinions is a prerequisite and, depending on personnel, not always that easy to achieve. It often doesn't happen on its own. A large part of a unified environment is the responsibility of the leaders in the locker room, but as I learned from American Hockey League (AHL) coach Roy Sommer, a coach can greatly enhance the situation.

Sommer is currently the longest-tenured coach in the AHL for the San Jose Sharks affiliate, currently in Worcester, Massachusetts. I was lucky to be a player and assistant coach with Sommer in the East Coast Hockey League (ECHL). He is a master at getting players to play hard for him and at creating a comfortable give-and-take culture in the locker room. I don't know if that's just the way he is or if he consciously tries to create that environment, but there is always a great feeling in his locker room. Players have fun and feel comfortable voicing their opinions, and the main reason for this is the way Sommer operates.

Sommer would always write a quote on the board before games, and he still does today. The quote seldom had anything directly to do with hockey but could always be applied to the team or the present situation in some way. Other coaches do this too, but what made this so effective for Sommer is how he encouraged conversation among the players about the quote and what it meant. I used to think he just wanted to get a certain message across, but now I know he did it for much more than that. It was a technique to effectively manage the environment. The result was a very comfortable atmosphere with greater buy-in from everyone on the team. With the players feeling comfortable and even encouraged to speak up, Sommer wasn't just getting information for that particular quote, but also setting the stage and creating an atmosphere to get buy-in for seasonal goals, not just game goals.

COMMUNICATING YOUR MISSION

You can't just make a statement at the start of the year about your goals and mission and expect to have it followed for the entire season. You have to revisit it, maybe tweak it, but certainly continue to stress it. Sommer's quotes were a method he used to create atmosphere, obtain better buy-in, and reinforce his message and mission. Since the message probably won't change much during the course of the season, it can be tedious to feed your team the same diet day after day.

Find ways to communicate a consistent mission in different ways. Mike Sertich (Minnesota Duluth, Michigan Tech) once said that if he could do it all over again he would be more himself. And Brad Buetow (Minnesota, San Diego, Colorado College) said something very similar—that he would allow his teams to see his human side. Dave Allison had a unique (and courageous) way of presenting his ideas that also allowed the team to see his human side, which I think is a benefit. Allison, who went on to be the head coach of the Ottawa Senators, wasn't afraid to put himself out there in the ways he motivated the team. He would do almost anything in team meetings or pregame speeches to keep his message fresh. He would march like a soldier, pat his head and rub his belly while he was giving his speech, or do any number of skits to get his message across. His method was uncommon and took courage, but it was very effective. As a player, what I loved about Allison was that I was always waiting to see what he would do next. It really kept my attention, and over the course of a long season that's extremely important. Even if the underlying message was the same, Allison's delivery made it fresh. Though I might not always have the courage to take the same approach, I keep that lesson in mind and try to keep my delivery original and compelling.

Communication is much better received when you speak positively. That keeps you focused on what you should do, not on what you shouldn't do. Stating that we will keep our feet moving keeps the focus on what we want to do. Saying we won't take any lazy stick penalties is referring to essentially the same goal, but it focuses on what not to do.

SETTING GOALS

Setting goals is also a common and effective way to communicate your mission to the team. There are many ways to go about this process, but if you're not confident in your own approach to setting and evaluating goals, try the widely accepted SMART method, which posits that goals should be specific, measureable, attainable, realistic, and timely:

Specific: Goals should be simply defined.

Measurable: To properly evaluate progress toward a goal, the goal has to be quantitatively measured. Simply saying, "We will work out more" is not measurable, so it's difficult to judge whether you're improving. This is very different from "We are going to add two cardio bike workouts of 30 minutes twice a week."

Attainable and Realistic: Having a goal that you can see yourself approaching and achieving is much more motivating than one that is beyond your reach.

Timely: A goal shouldn't be left open ended. Using the previous example, stating that you do two 30-minute cardio workouts per week is measurable and keeps you accountable, compared with "We will work out more."

Two rules I keep in mind when setting goals are to state the goal in positive terms and to have a goal that I can definitely control.

Athletes can be motivated by their own statistical goals. I think that's entirely up to the individual. But the goals I'm most interested in are the ones the athlete controls, or process goals as opposed to result goals. For example, if a player says his goal is to score 20 goals, I want to see what he is going to do to achieve that. Is he shooting 50 pucks after every practice or focusing on hitting the net on every shot in practice? Simply stating the result, without an emphasis on how to achieve that result, can turn into a depressing reminder if the results aren't immediately realized.

It's important that players come up with their own goals, but a team goal-setting session is critical as well and certainly helps the buy-in aspect of what you're trying to do. This session will probably be similar to the previous mission statement session. To make it effective, everyone should have a complete understanding of the team mission statement and be committed to coming up with goals that can be evaluated or measured to establish progress.

REINFORCING THE MESSAGE

Shortly after the beginning of the season, you should have evaluated your program and come up with a solid idea of what you want it to look like. You should have a mission or vision statement that your team has agreed on along with individual and team goals that support that statement. In my mind, this is the appetizer to the main meal. Being consistent in your message, being well organized, and having specific goals in mind for every meeting and every practice are essential if you want to maximize the development of your team. Basically it's walking the talk. The self-evaluation, the mission statement, the goal setting, are all important, but by no means is the job done. The most important part of communicating your mission is that you reinforce it every day.

This approach is a little different from the one I had when I started coaching. Several years into my coaching career, I focused primarily on the Xs and Os of hockey. I had an idea of the result I wanted, and our team would go through a goal-setting session. But the bulk of what we spent our time on was developing skills and incorporating those skills into systems. I believed if we could do an excellent job in those two areas, everything else would fall into place. As far as the on-ice product and criteria that I controlled, those two points were ranked number 1 and number 2, and nothing else came close. That philosophy changed when I was presented with a unique opportunity soon after arriving at Princeton in 2004. That was the year of the NHL lockout, and Ken Hitchcock, the head coach for the Philadelphia Flyers at the time, agreed to help the Princeton hockey program as a volunteer coach.

Having won a Stanley Cup, world championship, and Olympic gold medals, Hitchcock had a well-deserved reputation as a hockey systems genius. I was extremely excited to learn about his on-ice philosophies and systems. As I pestered him about specific systems, I was surprised when Hitchcock told me the aspect of coaching he is most passionate about is formulating team chemistry and having everyone working toward a common goal (or as the title of this chapter would suggest, communicating a team mission). We certainly did learn about systems and on-ice philosophies, but the biggest impact Hitchcock had on our program was what we learned about team building and how to effectively communicate our ideas to the players.

Before getting into the specifics of what we learned, I'd be remiss if I didn't first say that Hitchcock could not have been more generous with his time and knowledge. He'd watch video of the away games he couldn't attend and would come to the rink three and a half hours early if I had any questions about any of his material. He couldn't have been a more giving person, and our entire staff benefited greatly from his efforts. After the lockout ended, Hitchcock even invited us to attend the Flyers' camp and observe his practices, meetings, and video sessions. It was fun to see the lessons we learned applied to players at the highest level, and also to see those players execute the different drills we used to achieve specific results in practice. I have the ultimate respect for Hitchcock as a hockey coach, but even more respect for him as a person. I'm extremely proud of the success we enjoyed at Princeton, and Hitchcock deserves as much of the credit for that as anyone.

Hitchcock started with an end in mind. He wanted to know, and was respectful of, the way we communicated the message to the team. I was eager to compare on-ice systems and to decipher why certain systems were better than others. Later in the season, Hitchcock spent considerable time answering systems questions and talking about on-ice philosophies, but at the start of the season, Hitch refused to answer those questions. Instead, he asked the questions. He insisted on learning about our goals for the program and how we saw our team in the long term. Similar to our Geneva Convention regarding on-ice play, Hitchcock wanted to know all about our philosophies, objectives, and short- and long-term team goals before he shared his opinions about on-ice systems. He certainly followed some of the techniques we've discussed, but his attention to consistently reinforcing the team message was where our program benefited the most.

ORGANIZING THE TEAM COUNCIL

Once we clearly defined our philosophy, objectives, and vision, aside from refining our on-ice play, Hitchcock began introducing ideas on how to effectively communicate that vision to the team. Hitchcock joined us after our initial meetings, so his suggestions were geared toward walking the talk and consistently reinforcing our message. His first suggestion was to instruct 25 but coach 5. He introduced the idea of having a council, a group of players known as the five, that you have more detailed discussions with. Then it is that group's responsibility to direct the group.

The idea of a council sounds pretty basic. Hitchcock cautioned, however, that you need to get the right people on that council or it won't be effective. The council can't consist of just the players the coaching staff wants. It must include the players who have influence on the team. He supported this idea with stories about his own experiences when he felt strongly about who were his team leaders, only to later learn that the team felt differently and that transferring the power to the correct person meant a world of difference. In fact, Hitchcock said he would designate a coach on his staff to observe the team dynamics and document where the power of influence was.

Hitchcock was also very big on asking courageous questions, even to the point of purposely creating an uncomfortable situation for the sake of seeing who would step up to say what others wouldn't. The courageous questions were often directed at the coaching staff. Hitchcock told us if we didn't take that feedback personally, we would learn a great deal. I must admit, it was a little uncomfortable at first, but in the end he was absolutely correct.

We figured out how to identify team leaders and gave the council a try. The council had at least one representative from every position and at least one representative from every class. Our staff made decisions based on the makeup of the council and what aspects of the program the council would comment on. The group immediately took ownership in the program, and some of the best suggestions for positive change were implemented by this council. We experimented with transferring more ownership in different areas of our program and found this technique was effective. We also found other areas of responsibility that we wanted to retain for the coaching staff alone. We eventually established common ground that we all seemed comfortable with. This group proved to be instrumental in terms of communicating our mission and philosophies for a few reasons:

- The members of the council seemed more comfortable having challenging conversations within a smaller group.
- Council members were given the charge of being the voice of others, so they were more apt to make statements or ask questions because they were doing so on behalf of others.
- Council members felt ownership in decisions and therefore were more motivated to follow through with implementation.

RUNNING PRACTICES

Another aspect of Hitchcock's coaching repertoire that had a big impact in communicating a team mission was simply how he ran practices. It was immediately evident that Hitchcock would never run a drill that didn't comply with the mission or objectives he set out to achieve that day. That approach, in turn, perfectly reflected the end result and missions and objectives for the season and program. The entire season I never saw him run one drill just for fun or one that didn't comply exactly with the overall team mission and the specific objective of the practice. He told me that every day he strives for the perfect practice, and after watching him for a season, I believe he worked hard to achieve that goal.

Hitchcock often told us, "Games are [the players'] time; practice is my time." Every practice had a goal. Every drill had an exact purpose and was designed to achieve that goal. When Hitchcock didn't get the result he wanted for a particular drill, he was clearly disappointed and wouldn't proceed with his practice plan until he received the desired result or ran out of ice time. The consistency in how Hitchcock approached practice every day was vital to his ability to communicate the mission to everyone on the team. I believe actions speak much louder than words, and practice is an excellent platform to let your actions relay your mission.

CONCLUSION

Certainly there are many aspects of coaching. Communicating your mission to your team is one of the most important ones. I hope some of the ideas in this chapter will help you develop a mission, communicate that mission, and make your team better as a result. Have fun with it.

Acting as a Professional

Mike Schafer

One of the most common phrases used by coaches, and one of the highest compliments a coach can give is, "He is a real pro, on and off the ice." But what does this statement really mean? What does it mean to be a professional or act as a professional?

Being a professional can mean different things to different people. In fact, the definition of *professional* can have several meanings, including someone who is highly skilled, a person who works or performs for payment, or a person who belongs to a profession. Looking at what skills a hockey coach ought to have or the job the coach must perform is important for understanding how a coach should act in order to be considered a professional.

AHCA CODE OF CONDUCT

In fields such as education, medicine, and law, professional organizations establish standards of conduct for their members so they will act with a level of ethical behavior that the overall membership determines is appropriate. This ensures that members of these organizations perform with excellence and are accountable for their actions. For a college hockey coach, the guiding organization is the American Hockey Coaches Association.

Being involved in an organization allows us to keep an eye on the big picture. If we belong, we must get involved with the organization itself. A boss once told me, "It is your duty to serve the organization at least once, to help it run or improve." A professional needs to respond to the organization's requests in a timely fashion. A professional will volunteer when asked to help. If every member took the motto "leave things better than you found them" to heart, organizations would continue to grow and prosper.

Courtesy of Ned Dykes.

The AHCA developed a code of conduct that provides a blueprint of the responsibilities members have as professionals. The code of conduct includes the following:

- Responsibility to the game
- Responsibility to the institution and the student-athletes
- Responsibility to the officials
- Responsibility for public relations

I will touch on different areas in the code of conduct for college hockey coaches and how these areas of concern may affect the advancement of a coach's career and the development of the coach's skills and knowledge. Members of the AHCA must understand the code of conduct and then base all their actions on the larger picture of what the organization believes in. Let's start with responsibility to the game.

Responsibility to the Game

All driven professionals want to be successful in business or sport. In athletics, "win at all costs" is a motto that cannot and should not be tolerated. Coaches are role models, and we have a responsibility to respect the game itself. I believe this starts with what our sport stands for. The game of hockey has always been a fast, up-tempo sport with exciting displays of skill combined with a physical element that is unique compared with all other sports. Skating, shooting, and passing plus hockey sense and vision combined with the physical strength and mental toughness to play the game have defined hockey since its inception. As professionals, it is important that we respect the combination of skills and the history of the game.

We act unprofessionally when we coach in ways that affect this combination of skill and physical presence or try to influence rule changes. A clear example of this is when coaches encourage or accept players' diving to draw penalties or faking injuries to draw more severe penalties.

At the other end of the spectrum is the use of obstruction to negate the skill of an opponent or the use of excessive force or lack of discipline to interfere with the flow of the game. We must self-evaluate to see if our team is the most penalized in the league or if we are part of a staff that yells and complains every time someone hits or bumps our players. At all levels of hockey, some people will do whatever they think they need to do in order to win. But playing by the rules and maintaining respect for the game in all facets of teaching will earn us the compliment of being professional because we've lived up to that standard.

With respect to the game, it's not always the written rules that identify a professional. Failure to observe the unwritten rules—the spirit of the game—usually results in a coach losing the respect of peers within the coaching community. Does the coach keep his top power play on the ice even while holding a large lead against the opponent? With that large lead, does he play it out and respect the opponent? When a game is out of reach, does the team play with discipline? Does the coach discipline his players for hitting from behind, for kneeing someone, or for trying to embarrass an opponent? Does the coach encourage trash talking, which shows a lack of respect for the opponent?

Many leagues have clearly articulated policies regarding treatment of opponents and officials in a team's home facility. These might include providing clean locker room facilities, producing a quality copy of the game video, and responding to appropriate requests from a visiting team. We are responsible for providing a first-class experience for off-ice and on-ice officials, media, and fans.

These are just a few examples of situations in which coaches have opportunities to live up to their responsibilities and respect the game. Our actions will help determine the level of professionalism we achieve. When we come up short in any of these areas in an attempt to benefit our team, we have not performed in a manner that our organization demands of coaches.

Responsibility to the Institution and the Student-Athletes

Most members of the AHCA belong to an academic institution. We serve the institution and its vision. We are not simply coaches but educators as well. Our responsibility is to hold athletes accountable for their actions and performance at the institution, inside and outside the hockey arena. Low grade point averages (GPAs), poor classroom attendance, poor behavior, and poor graduation rates all reflect on the coach.

We must uphold our responsibility to the institution to make sure our athletes take full advantage of their academic opportunities. Coaches hold the ultimate motivational card—playing time—when athletes aren't holding up their end in terms of academic performance. Athletes want to play, but we decide who gets ice time. The coach who plays this card for the greater good of the student-athlete is being a responsible educator.

As a professional, the coach must make sure that policies within the department are followed regarding meetings, administrative meetings, deadlines, and so on. The institution must be held in the highest regard. A coach must have a well-established set of standards that is clearly and consistently communicated to the players and staff. These standards indicate what situations must be reported to university officials because of department policy. When the coach becomes aware of any type of misconduct that is against the team's standards, whether from players, coaches, alumni, or boosters, the proper officials within the institution must be notified immediately.

Student-athletes should be treated like our own sons or daughters. We want our children to develop ideals and character traits that we can be proud of. The safety and welfare of our children and their friends should never be jeopardized, and neither should the safety and welfare of our athletes and their competitors. When our children misbehave, or our athletes exhibit unsportsmanlike conduct, it is our responsibility to ensure that behavior isn't repeated. If we treat our players in the same way we would treat our own children, we have the basis of acting as professionals with regard to our relationships with our athletes.

Responsibility to the Officials

Coaches must treat officials, members of the media, and all support staff with respect, honesty, and courtesy. All these individuals are attempting to service the game itself, not us as coaches. The referee holds the coaches and players accountable for their actions so the game can be played according to the rules. The media is there to report what happened during the game. The off-ice officials are there to ensure the game is run properly and safely for everyone. Coaches are responsible for making sure all these people are treated with respect at all times.

Responsibility for Public Relations

Coaches must take advantage of opportunities for public relations to highlight their own institution, the opponent's institution, and the game itself. Coaches often miss tremendous professional opportunities to compliment an opponent or coach for a good game or to praise the performance of their own players. When a coach wins, it is easy to hold to the professional standards that everyone expects. A true professional is judged by how he handles defeat.

PERSONAL CHARACTERISTICS OF PROFESSIONALS

Now that we have identified the AHCA's beliefs, what other areas of the coaching world are important when being judged? When we talk about being professional or running a professional organization, what characteristics are easily identifiable?

A professional doesn't expect to be paid by the hour. Early in my career, I was told to never add up the hours and figure out my hourly rate because I would always be disappointed. We are paid to get the job done. It is important to know your job description and all your responsibilities, and then as a professional you must fulfill those responsibilities.

A professional must be able to follow through and work independently once she is shown how to do things. Once a person is taught the proper way to perform and is given the resources to be successful, that person earns the label of professional when she is able to perform with excellence with a minimum of supervision. For example, a strong assistant coach can follow through with projects and assignments without much supervision, performing like a head coach.

Another defining characteristic is that a professional doesn't consider himself a boss but rather a supervisor who is part of a team. In our relationships with assistants, administrative assistants, trainers, equipment managers, alumni groups, and players, we should see ourselves as guiding the ship instead of being the boss. We will be regarded as a professional leader as opposed to a justified dictator.

Once we take into consideration all the views and knowledge that the organization can provide, a leader must make decisions on who plays, who is recruited, what changes are made to the system, what equipment is ordered, who performs what responsibilities within the program, and so on. Once those decisions are made, a leader must accept the responsibility for any subsequent issues and not attempt to assign blame for mistakes to others.

Two more important aspects of professionalism are confidentiality and trust. An assistant coach must respect conversations that occur between himself and players, but also be loyal to the head coach. A head coach must support his assistant with regard to recruiting or in dealing with players. A head coach must respect the confidentiality of players with regard to a host of issues such as academics, injury, or alcohol use. An administrative assistant must understand that team issues should never be discussed with anyone.

As a rule, confidentiality within the team and university must never be violated. However, it is imperative that the staff and the team be aware of all the standards and policies. This type of communication has to be exceedingly clear to every single player and staff member, so they know exactly when a coach has no choice but to report misconduct.

Moral and Ethical Behavior

As a professional, when you give your word, it should be fulfilled. Therefore, always be careful of what you say. Morality is a weighty issue in athletics from a recruiting standpoint. Problems arise, for example, when a student-athlete is promised a spot on the team and that spot never materializes. When a gentlemen's agreement exists, that agreement should be honored. Avoid promises that can't be fulfilled athletically or academically. Coaches shouldn't break the rules when talking to or calling juniors or by watching a player more often than is allowed. Coaches shouldn't engage in negative recruiting against a school by spreading rumors or putting doubt in a student's mind based on inaccurate information.

Recruitment is an area in which many assistant and head coaches go astray. They fail to understand that they are not only acting unprofessionally, but also hurting their chances of advancing. When you are running a program, morality and values are characteristics that will either haunt you or help you.

Professional Growth

A true professional is always trying to improve. Coaches must continually evaluate what they're doing and how they're doing it. They must be open to criticism and be able to accept suggestions as an opportunity to improve, not as a personal attack. They must be open with assistant coaches and able to communicate with them to see if change is needed. They need the perspective of players. Coaches then should be able to adjust based on that feedback, provided it fits into their philosophy for success. They must attend clinics, watch practices of other teams, talk and share with other coaches in order to refine, change, and improve. They must be willing to read books on motivation, leadership, and management while keeping an eye on who they really are. They must continue to self-evaluate and improve in order to be true professionals.

Consider the medical field. Those in medicine are required to keep learning throughout their careers as new treatments and technologies are developed. We expect medical professionals to feel a moral obligation to care for us using the most effective ways. In a similar way, hockey coaches should work hard to continue to improve their sport knowledge, leadership skills, and ability to motivate in order to better their teams, protect their players, and grow their programs.

Throughout your career, continue to be active in your development as a professional. Nurture your skills and knowledge. If you think you don't need to attend a clinic, read books, or speak to others about their successes, you've stopped advancing as a professional. Although we must be true to ourselves, communication skills can always improve, game knowledge can improve, and management of time and others can improve. In many areas of our lives, we can affect our surroundings for the better. We must always strive to develop and grow.

A professional will also be careful not to advance at the expense of others. Hockey is such a small world, and there are many competitive, driven coaches who would love to be head coaches at the collegiate, junior, or professional levels. In the unstable world of coaching, where things can and will go wrong, true professionals are loyal to their coworkers, supervisors, and players. Inevitably coaches will sometimes find themselves disagreeing with how policies are made or how players are coached. Be aware that insubordination can taint your career for the rest of your life, so act accordingly.

It amazes me to hear some coaches talk about their staff, their players, or other issues with their programs. Those conversations lead me to make a mental note to never trust or hire those coaches. Coaches with aspirations of taking over certain jobs will sometimes speak to athletic department members and drop subtle hints that things aren't going well. Professionals must be loyal at all times to the team in all conversations with athletes, department members, alumni, and others. If you're unable to be 100 percent loyal at all times, you should remove yourself from the situation in order to maintain your status as a professional.

Falling prey to rumor and hearsay is one temptation many coaches can't resist. After returning from the road one time, I reported to my head coach that I thought a school was recruiting a player illegally. I spoke with some other coaches about it and believed something should be done. My head coach promptly told me unless I was willing to confront the person involved, it should never be mentioned again. In other words, rumors alone weren't sufficient. I needed to be able to substantiate my suspicions. Again, being involved in hearsay and rumor hinders our ability to be considered professional.

Professional Advancement

Advancing as a professional in the coaching field can be very difficult but also very rewarding. Unfortunately, one person's joy is usually another's sorrow. The coaching fraternity can be close at times, and it's always difficult when someone loses a job he loves. As coaches, we know there comes a time when most of us will be replaced. If you never are, you can consider yourself one of the fortunate. When advancing as a coach, acting as a professional is the biggest factor in gaining a reputation you can carry into any situation. Seeing how coaches handle themselves in game situations, when recruiting, and at social events provides an important glimpse into their character.

It takes a lifetime to develop a reputation but only one brief moment to destroy it, and hockey is such a small world. Many assistant coaches become head coaches, head coaches move on to become athletic directors or take other administrative positions, but they all carry their reputations with them. Understand that you will be in contact with many people throughout your career. When I call an institution for scheduling or other information, it always surprises me to find someone there who has a connection to hockey. Acting like a professional is key to advancing in the profession.

Have a plan for yourself and map out your career. Be comfortable in your plans for advancement with regard to yourself and your family. Be realistic in what you are willing to do, where you are willing to live, who you are willing to work for, and what you want to stand for. Once you set those parameters, you can begin the pursuit of your career. Along the way, don't be afraid to solicit letters of support from people who can verify your professional standards. This can be very helpful when applying for jobs later on, indicating you have support from respected people in the profession. Don't be afraid to sit down, reevaluate, and change your plan as your personal life changes.

Be ready to work for different people so you can develop you own ideas of how you want to run your program when you get the opportunity. Seeing how people handle different situations with regard to coaching, managing the bench, and recruiting is invaluable as you journey through your career.

In the pursuit of career advancement, you must be willing to persevere. It's going to be a long road for most. Find ways to enjoy both the journey and the present, knowing that you must persevere over time in order to achieve your career goals. This is the biggest reason for turnover in the coaching business. As mentioned earlier, as professionals we must understand that we aren't paid by the hour. If we enter the profession comfortable with the notion that financial gain is unlikely for a long time, we are better able to persevere in order to reach our career goals.

Like any other business, it is crucial to network as you move along your career path. This includes speaking to coaches on the road and introducing yourself to head coaches. Investing sincere time in speaking to those in the business will expose you to many people who might help you advance and also provide opportunities to learn new ideas, drills, and skills that can aid your development as a coach and as a person. If you handle yourself professionally and are sincere, networking will give you the opportunity to showcase your talents to others.

For advancement, there is no substitute for developing a reputation as a tireless worker, someone who does her due diligence in any task. I earned more respect at a hockey school that had five attending head coaches than in any other situation in my career. By taking the initiative to do things right, not needing supervision, being able to deliver a quality experience for players with the head coaches present, and volunteering to do jobs that others didn't want, I gained the respect of people who could help me later in my career. A solid work ethic and professionalism go hand in hand.

Many young coaches benefit from seeking out a mentor, someone to help navigate the early stages of a career. When advancing as a professional, it helps to be able to relate to someone who can bring perspective to your professional and personal lives. Find someone who can be a sounding board, who is willing to challenge you personally to make change, and who is honest because he knows it will help and that you won't be offended.

CONCLUSION

Acting as a professional is a difficult subject to cover in one chapter. It is even more difficult to do for a lifetime. We will make mistakes, and many of us will have moments in which we don't live up to the expectations of our profession or our own values. However, a true professional knows when to take responsibility for his actions, is able to apologize, and is able to do the right thing in order to rectify any problem or situation.

5

Gaining Community and Parent Support

Marty Palma

Here you are, head coach of a hockey team. As we all know, coaching is a full-time job. The thought and preparation that go into a season can become very stressful. Coaches have to worry about recruiting players, evaluating them during training camp, and then choosing which combination of players provides the best chance of building a winning team.

Coaches have to prepare for practices, consider line combinations, study which skills players need to work on or develop, learn each player's personality, teach the troops to play within the system, put together power-play and penalty-killing units, and facilitate what needs to be done to be successful, both on and off the ice. Coaches need to think about game-day matchups, which goaltender is starting, what to do if someone gets injured, how to keep the team focused, and how to deal with any adversity the team may face throughout the season.

That's a lot of work. But many other components may not be anticipated when a coach signs up to coach a hockey team, aspects such as marketing, fund-raising, selling tickets and apparel, and scheduling, just to name a few. The size of the program will determine the coach's level of involvement with the business or nonhockey operations of the organization. Whether your program is large or small, you're ultimately responsible for how it is run.

In this chapter, we'll explore the noncoaching challenges coaches face. We'll answer the following questions: What are some of the differences between a large program and a small program? What types of support are needed to make a program successful? What is the importance of this support and how can a coach obtain it? The answers will help you build a strong team foundation and create a winning organization or solidify an already successful club.

LARGE PROGRAMS VERSUS SMALL PROGRAMS

A major program may have many resources for organizational operations and most likely a large operating budget. Examples include an NCAA Division I college team or a large junior program. Most coaches in these types of programs coach as their full-time job, and the challenges they face are typically confined to the team they put on the ice. They have to research and recruit good players who are also good students. These coaches still have to worry about operating the team efficiently and effectively, but most of the behind-the-scenes operations are managed by others.

However, there's much more to running a successful club than meets the eye. The coach of a large program might need to work with a support staff that handles various responsibilities. For example, the leagues that larger clubs participate in usually take care of scheduling referees, while smaller programs might have to do that job on their own.

Major programs may have a team manager whose duties include scheduling games, scheduling game-time employees and volunteers, and arranging the team's transportation and lodging. The team manager may write and distribute press releases and ensure that any required paperwork is filled out and filed appropriately and promptly. The team manager also makes certain, if necessary, that players meet QPA and GPA requirements for eligibility purposes.

A large program might have a marketing team that promotes the organization, creating different ways to generate publicity. All this work is accomplished via a substantial operating budget that allows them to function for the season.

Coaches of small programs may sometimes wish they could just worry about coaching the hockey team. Many of the behind-the-scenes tasks are viewed as hurdles that must be overcome every year. Being in charge of a small program is usually considered a part-time job even though it takes the same hours as a full-time job to accomplish everything that needs to be done. When leading a small program, coaches have to wear many different hats. They are the team's coach as well as the team manager, the marketing department, the web designer, the graphic artist, the team spokesperson, and even the accounting department.

Furthermore, coaches of small programs need to take on these tasks within the constraints of a limited budget. Being creative in finding ways to complete each task is key to being successful. Trying to do everything yourself can be overwhelming and exhausting, so building a support team to help with the operation of the organization is imperative.

Understanding the costs associated with a program can shed light on why it's important to have help. Conservatively, it costs a small program between $35,000 and $40,000 to run the team effectively. Most small organizations will probably need to raise between $25,000 and $30,000 to make ends meet, or they may even have to come up with the full amount. To help alleviate some of the headaches and expenses, the coach should work to gain support from the parents and community. If you're coaching a high school team, club team, or Division II or Division III collegiate team, gaining needed support will take thorough planning on your part. But, in the end, it will be well worth your efforts.

PARENT SUPPORT

One of the most important ingredients required for a successful program, small or major, is parental support. The last thing any coach wants is to have the parents involved in the operation of the team, but let's face it: Most parents will do anything to help their children. Parents are the start of your team's fan base and a crucial part of your team's success. Engage the parents. Even though parent involvement is a challenge for most coaches, if you recruit parents in a constructive way, they can carry much of the burden that goes along with running the team.

If you don't actively seek out parental support, you'll likely be saddled with 100 percent of a team's off-ice responsibilities. However, if you gain the support of parents, you can reduce your off-ice contribution to around 20 percent (figure 5.1). So what is the best way to accomplish this?

You can always send a basic form letter asking parents for their help and support, but letters can get filed away without ever being read. To grab

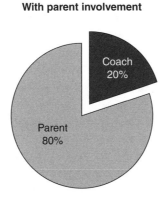

With parent involvement

FIGURE 5.1 Enlisting the support of parents reduces the coach's off-ice contribution to running the team to about 20 percent.

the parents' attention, hold a formal meeting. Be sure to set up the meeting on a day and at a time that works for most parents, even if it means changing dates and rearranging your schedule to accommodate them, and let parents know their participation is important. The more people that show up, the better chance you have of gaining their support. Make certain your coaching staff and the athletic director are present as well. This way, parents can see that everyone in the system, from top to bottom, is on the same page, and you're making this a team endeavor.

Start by telling the parents about your coaching style. Let them know what your expectations are for the season. Show them the passion and the dedication you have for the program. Next, detail the expenses of running the team. Be up front, specifying how much effort is required to help their children and the team succeed. Encourage the parents to be part of the organization. This will help you establish a good relationship with them, and it will help both you and the program succeed.

At the meeting, identify particular tasks that need to be done every year in order for the team to do well. Focus on identifying parents who are willing to handle game-day tasks. Possibly the most important job is to have parents establish and commit to a fund-raising committee.

For home games, parent volunteers can be responsible for a number of key game-day tasks that bring in revenue to help offset any budget shortfalls, such as admissions, 50/50 raffle tickets, and team apparel sales. Having the parents take ownership by volunteering for these tasks can make for a successful game-day operation and a less stressful time for you.

Next, establish a fund-raising committee to take charge of generating revenue. A stable fund-raising committee can be beneficial for years. Provide an outline of fund-raising ideas to guide the members, including but not limited to weekly or monthly raffles, food sales, candy sales, and car washes. Suggest that the parents contact local professional teams to ask for donated items or event tickets to raffle off. This is one way to start gaining valuable community involvement, which will be discussed in greater detail later. Ask the parents for their input, too. They might have ideas you did not think of or list on the form.

Keep in mind that even though you have delegated fund-raising, you can't completely distance yourself from it. You still have to monitor it and make yourself available if the parents have questions or need assistance. A fund-raising committee will allow you to spend more time coaching, which is part of the goal you're trying to achieve by delegating. Plus, it's a way to reach out and gain the support and involvement of the parents.

COMMUNITY SUPPORT

Community support is vital for the success of your organization. There are two types of communities: internal and external. The internal community consists of students and staff members at your school. The external community consists of local newspapers, radio stations, businesses, and foundations. Gaining these resources will require some work on your part, but it is well worth the effort.

Internal Community

Among the assets of your internal community are the students. By working closely with the athletic director and guidance counselors from your school, you can find dependable student volunteers who are interested in helping the team. For example, perhaps a sports management major can act as the team manager and help with the day-to-day operations of the team.

Under your direction, student volunteers can help with scheduling, distribute and collect paperwork, disseminate important information to the players, assist parent volunteers with their game-day projects, and act as the team liaison between you and the school and you and the parents. These students can help complete the fundamental work that needs to be accomplished throughout the season while gaining the necessary organizational and time-management skills needed to excel in their chosen fields.

Students studying graphic design can design announcements, posters, and brochures to promote the team and also create programs that can be sold at games. This is another way to reach out and gain more community involvement.

A student majoring in web design can add some professionalism to the organization by starting and maintaining a team website. Using one of the many free website companies available, the web designer can build a site that creates awareness and support for your team.

A journalism student can follow the team through the year, writing articles for the school newspaper. He can interview players, coaches, and fans, which will draw people to the team. Be sure your student reporter includes contact information at the end of each article so anyone interested in helping the team can get in touch with you. This may be a gateway to even more support.

Using this part of your internal community will benefit not only you, the team, and the parents involved, but also the volunteering students by providing the opportunity to gain valuable experience and possibly credit toward their majors.

The next type of internal support is school staff members. Gaining the support of faculty members, the athletic director, the dean, and even the school president can help elevate the program on campus and beyond. Having faculty members involved can lead to a larger fan base, while the athletic director, the dean, and the president can ensure the program flourishes for years to come. These people are also instrumental in the process of allocating money for the team budget. Increasing the support you need from the internal community will help you transform your small program into something special, accomplishing your goal of having a successful organization.

Finally, there is one vital component of the internal community that every coach has but often overlooks—the players. The players form a crucial link between the team and the members of the internal and external communities. Players bring in family and friends who might not otherwise have been involved with the program, thereby increasing game-day attendance and revenues. These same people will be there to support the team's fund-raising efforts. It is also a great idea to offer family and friends a season pass discount. This will enable you to build up the fan base for your games.

From the start of the season, the coach must stress to the players that their involvement is necessary not only to the team on the ice but to the organization as a whole. Players must be willing to participate in all fund-raising efforts. You can make the fund-raising mandatory for the entire team, but a better idea is to make players want to participate. For example, you can offer incentives for the highest sales. Or you can divide players into fund-raising teams, and the group that sells the most magazines gets team hats or shirts. This will motivate players to participate and set a goal to help them execute their fund-raising efforts.

Your internal support team is made up of students, faculty, staff, and players. To ignore any one of these components would be a mistake. Using all of them not only makes your job as coach easier but also benefits your organization as a whole.

External Support

External support can include local newspapers, businesses, foundations, and radio stations, all part of a supporting cast that can benefit the team as well as the community. Making the most of these resources is vital to your organization's future. External support is a good way to simultaneously shine a spotlight on your club and reach out to the larger community. It is geared toward connecting with people who aren't closely associated with the program but whose support can be significant.

Local Newspapers and Social Media

The local newspaper can be a relatively simple but highly effective asset when trying to gain community publicity and build fan support. Newspapers can publish tryout information to increase player attendance and circulate season schedules, game reports, and any special promotions the team is planning. This is a great way to get in contact with the community.

Today, in the internet age, an effective and easy way to promote your program is to employ social media. Creating a Facebook page or a Twitter account can help publicize your organization. Both of these resources can be used to provide real-time game scores, injury reports, photos, and even videos. This can help add excitement and a professional touch to your team.

Business Support

Local businesses are always looking for ways to promote their services, and one way to gain their support is to offer advertising packages. Whether it is a law firm, a doctor's office, a construction company, or a restaurant, business owners want to increase exposure. Advertising on hockey rink dasher boards is becoming an increasingly popular way for businesses to gain publicity and for your team to bring in revenue.

Of course, before approaching businesses, you'll need to meet with a sign company and your rink management to develop a plan that will benefit everyone involved. When you approach establishments, be able to provide the cost of advertising as well as statistics about how much exposure this type of marketing brings. Offer different packages to help business owners find the right advertising campaign. Emphasize that working together with the businesses in your area can be advantageous to all concerned.

Foundations and Radio Stations

One of the best ways to engage the community is to partner with a nonprofit foundation. For example, my hockey team played a benefit game for the Susan G. Komen organization for breast cancer awareness. Our players wore pink jerseys, and after the game they sold the shirts off their backs to help raise money for the foundation.

Because of that success, we decided to do a benefit game every year. Each year, we pick a new foundation to promote. This is also a good option for players who need to earn community service hours for graduation. Table 5.1 lists some of the many foundations you can work with to help your organization reach out to the community.

TABLE 5.1 Charitable Foundations

Alzheimer's Association	The Conservation Fund
American Heart Association	Juvenile Diabetes Research Foundation
American Kidney Fund	Leader Dogs for the Blind
American Parkinson Disease Association	Leukemia and Lymphoma Society
American Red Cross	March of Dimes Birth Defects Foundation
American Sudden Infant Death Syndrome Institute	Multiple Sclerosis Society
Central Association for the Blind and Visually Impaired	Susan G. Komen
Disabled American Veterans	The Parkinson Alliance

Before doing a benefit game, contact your local radio stations by email or telephone and provide details about what your team is trying to accomplish. Ask for their support and if they'll mention your event over the air. Emphasize that the game is being played for a good cause. You'll find that many stations are happy to accommodate you and your team. Benefit games not only increase attendance but also generate a sense of satisfaction for you and your players, knowing you were able to contribute to a worthy cause.

SHOW GRATITUDE

After receiving support from the parents, students, staff, players, newspapers, businesses, foundations, and radio stations, be sure to publicly thank them for their time, efforts, and assistance. Acknowledge and promote the accomplishments of the volunteer staff. Making an announcement at a game, publishing a commentary or open thank-you letter in the newspaper, or adding an article to your game program is a nice gesture to show your gratitude for everything they have done.

An even better way to show your thanks is to have a fan and sponsor appreciation game. Offer free or discounted admission, free food and drink, or giveaways to show how much you value what they've done for your team. Allowing them to see how much you appreciate their support can help you achieve the same level of assistance every year.

CONCLUSION

The many challenges coaches face while running a hockey program can be reduced with the help of people from both inside and outside the organization. Whether the coach is responsible for the success of a large or small program, he needs to obtain assistance from many people and groups and from many levels.

Setting a goal for yourself and establishing a plan are essential for your success and the success of your organization. Getting cooperation and involvement from parents, students, school staff and administrators, players, and your community from the beginning of the season will smooth the long road ahead.

Remember, you cannot be the only block in the foundation of the organization. The more blocks you have properly installed, the more stable that foundation will be. Building a sound relationship with your internal and external communities will help you achieve your goal, which is to have your organization be successful for years to come.

6

Building a
High School Program

Hal Tearse

Building a successful high school hockey program in Minnesota is no easy feat. Nearly every public high school in Minnesota has a team, and there is a rich hockey tradition that culminates each year with the state tournaments.

When I was asked to start a brand new program at Providence Academy in Plymouth, Minnesota, a school that was only four years old, I knew I had many obstacles to overcome. The essence of a program begins with great coaching, talented players, and ongoing support from the school. We quickly assembled a coaching staff, and we already had the support of the school. Having enough players to start a program was our first major challenge, and finding the right competitive level was the second. We decided to take the "build it and they will come" approach.

Minnesota lays claim to being the state of hockey, and it may be hard to argue against that. The NHL's Minnesota Wild are at the top of a system that includes five Division I college teams, nine Division III college programs, 165 high school programs, and more than 45,000 registered youth players. That's a great deal of hockey.

During the summer months of 2003, the local hockey association in Wayzata, Minnesota, proposed to add a third sheet of ice to the existing facility in Plymouth. The existing building is owned and operated by the city but was built with the help of the hockey association. The new proposal was a three-way effort with the hockey association, the city, and a new private school, Providence Academy. I attended the city council meeting to show support for the much-needed addition, as our program had nearly 1,000 registered players. Ice time was in short supply, and this third sheet of ice would help alleviate the problem. The proposal was approved in concept at the June meeting, with funding provided to contract the designers.

As I left the meeting, several gentlemen approached me and asked if I was interested in coaching the new high school team at Providence Academy. Having coached at every level of youth hockey, Division III college, the USHL, USA Hockey Selects, and the National Sports Festival over the past 30 years, I was ready for a new challenge. I replied that I was interested and that we should stay in touch.

I didn't think the new school would be able to play the next year. The reality of the situation was that without the new sheet of ice, there wouldn't be a team. We were only 16 months away from the season, and the rink was still in the planning stages. In March of 2004, after several minor setbacks and increased funding commitments from all three parties, construction began on the new ice sheet. A week after receiving the final approval to build, I was hired as the new coach after several candidates were interviewed.

Now the real work was about to begin. Providence administrators anticipated it would take years to build the program. They indicated that win–loss results were not important and, based on experience with their other young teams, understood that losses might be the primary statistic for the first few years. That's the kind of challenge I like.

Providence Academy is a Roman Catholic college preparatory school. Founded in 2001 on the principles of a strong faith-based education, core-knowledge curriculum, and virtue, the administrators believe that athletics are an important part of the educational process. However, high-quality academics is the primary focus. In that context, I set about to build a program from scratch.

My overall vision was to build a first-class program consistent with the school's overall commitment to excellence. We would soon have a new arena and great facilities for the players. Now we needed a staff of outstanding coaches to make sure the players developed and improved. I believe that playing high school hockey should be one of the best memories a player takes with him when he graduates. With all that in mind, I started to put all the pieces of the puzzle together.

COACHES

I believe a team is only as good as the assistant coaches, and I wanted the best. For a new team with young players, I wanted coaches who could help with fundamentals but could also coach the finer points of the game as the team matured over the next several years. Several people who wanted to join the staff contacted me, but I knew they were really only interested in being head coaches. I needed people I could trust, who were knowledge-able, and whom I could work with.

A friend recommended Andy Ness as a candidate. I had coached Andy at Augsburg College his freshman year and had seen him only a couple of times since. He was teaching physical education at a local Catholic school and was coaching the JV team at Hill Murray High School in St. Paul. Andy had also spent many years teaching skating at Pro Edge power skating school. I knew Andy was the right fit for the job, and he quickly agreed to join the staff.

I couldn't get my first choice to coach the defensemen, so I decided this position would remain unfilled for the first year, and I would look to fill the position in year two. I assumed those duties the first year.

For the goaltenders, I added Robb Stauber. Robb was a Hobey Baker Award winner in 1988 and a veteran NHL goalie. He is one of the finest goalie coaches in the country, and many of the goalies in town already worked with him. Robb was a natural fit for our program, and he lived in our community. He had worked with my bantam teams in the previous three years, and we worked well together.

The last coach I hired was Kirk Olson as our off-ice strength and quickness trainer. Kirk was a full-time employee of the Minnesota Wild in the same capacity. He worked on resistance training and conditioning with the boys several times a week after practice. We saw tremendous improvement in the team over the course of the season, and the boys really worked hard for him.

PLAYERS

Once the rink completion was assured, we needed to determine how many players we currently had in the school. With an enrollment in grades 9 through 12 of only 162 students at the time, we needed to get lucky. As it turned out, there were 16 players with various hockey backgrounds. Not all the boys were actually willing to participate, but we believed we had a chance to get the program started.

In May of 2004, I held an informational meeting for prospective players and their parents. Many of the players still had one more year of bantam eligibility and were not sure they wanted to be involved. Many knew me by reputation, but I didn't know any of them personally. It was like going on a blind date with 30 people, and they all want to get to know you. At the same time I was also sizing them up to determine if I had completely lost all touch with reality. I looked the boys over and thought that when they get a couple of years older, we may have a shot at being competitive.

In essence, I had to convince 15 players and their parents to believe in our program. They all had other options in the youth hockey system.

Although the boys already attended our school, it felt as if I was recruiting 15 new players at the same time.

At the meeting, I discussed my philosophy of hockey and the importance of strong academics. I stressed that preparation and skill development were the keys to any successful endeavor on and off the ice. We talked about pride, playing for the school, and being the pioneers of what I envisioned to be a high-quality program built on hard work, dedication, and discipline.

The meeting went as well as could be expected, but we still had one major problem: We didn't have a goaltender. Until I could solve that problem, the players were reluctant to commit to the program.

To get a line on a goaltender I called on Robb Stauber, who operates a training academy in Edina, Minnesota. He was a volunteer goalie coach for the University of Minnesota Gophers, and I had used his services for several years with our Tier 1 bantam team in Wayzata. He had agreed to be part of the staff, so now we needed him to help locate a goalie.

As it turned out, Robb knew of a high school senior goaltender, Brett Anderson, who was working at his Goalcrease Academy. Brett had been squeezed out of his high school team because of an overabundance of net minders. Since we were going to play a JV schedule in our first year, we were not restricted by the Minnesota State High School League rules that require that all players attend the school. Brett agreed to be our goaltender and drive the 25 miles from Buffalo to Plymouth each day for practices and games. We could not have selected a finer young man to anchor our team. Now that we had a goalie, it was time to get commitments from the other players.

We gathered again as a group. The boys spent time in the pool and ate copious amounts of food while I visited with the parents for several hours. One big advantage of our program, from the perspective of the parents, was that we practiced right after school, and the boys would be home by 6:30 p.m. for family dinner and homework. Most bantam and older youth teams in the metro area are assigned 8:30 to 10:30 p.m. ice slots, and the boys often get home after 11:00. The parents were soon on board, and the players committed to the program.

We ended up with nine boys in 9th grade, two in 10th, and two in 12th grade for a total of 13 players. With the addition of our new goalie, we had a roster of 14. I was very confident we would not have any complaints about lack of ice time, but I was worried about injuries and illness and not having enough players to participate. Fortunately, neither affected us.

SCHEDULING GAMES

High school teams in Minnesota are allowed to play a maximum of 25 games, plus qualifying playoffs, during a 16-week season. Nearly every high school is in a conference that accounts for the majority of their regular season schedule. The conference that Providence Academy participates in didn't have hockey, so I was left with the task of scheduling all our games.

Because we had a new program, the competition wasn't lining up to pencil us in. I spent a couple of months calling coaches, asking them to play us at the JV level. A number of programs in the state don't field a JV team, thus leaving openings in the schedules of their conference rivals. Slowly, over the course of the summer, I was able to schedule about 15 games. We would add and drop games as the season progressed. One team scheduled two games with us and then canceled one, offered to schedule at another date, and then canceled the second game with two days' notice. I guess they got better offers. Another team accepted an invitation to play us in late February. As the date drew near, my attempts to confirm the date went unanswered. I eventually learned they had finished the season and turned in their equipment.

I had to rely on my friends and hockey connections to get teams to schedule games with our fledgling program. Wally Chapman, head coach at Breck School, was very gracious and scheduled three JV games and hosted a varsity scrimmage with our team. Greg Trebil, from AA powerhouse Academy of Holy Angels in Richfield, made room for us on their JV schedule. We were also lucky to get a spot in the Schwan Cup Holiday Tournament thanks to my friend Pete Carlson. Will Fish, the varsity coach from Owatonna, included our club in their November varsity preview and holiday JV tournament (which we won). As you can see, it helps to have friends in the hockey community when starting a new program.

EQUIPMENT AND LOCKER ROOMS

I had two major problems to resolve regarding our team equipment. The first was ordering enough equipment in sizes that would fit our players in the first year and also in subsequent years as the program matured along with the players. The second issue was where to store the equipment when it arrived, as the school didn't have space to store hockey gear and the rink was under construction.

The first issue was fairly easy to resolve. We ordered 30 sets of equipment in various sizes so we could accommodate almost every player. This worked well with the exception of having to order a size small in hockey pants for a player who was admitted to the school in late August.

The second issue was defaulted to my garage, where 40 cases and boxes of equipment resided for the better part of four months as we waited for the arena to be completed or the season to begin, whichever occurred first.

Locker rooms presented another challenge. The arrangement with the city was for the school to have two permanent team rooms, two coaches' locker rooms, and one equipment and skate-sharpening room. The city provided the space, and the school was responsible for building the rooms.

I had to design the rooms and then arrange for the lockers and other furnishings to be constructed. As we reviewed the blueprints, it became apparent that a few minor changes would improve the spaces a great deal. One change I requested was to combine the two very small coaches' locker rooms into one and add a bathroom and shower. This was accomplished at an additional cost, but the space is now much more usable.

I wanted the locker rooms to be a place where the players were comfortable and would want to spend time. The lockers needed to be functional, and the space had to be adequate to serve the needs of the team. I enlisted the help of one of the parents of a senior player to visit several other new rinks in the area and tour their locker rooms. I asked him to photograph the lockers at Gustavus College in Northfield, as we had determined their locker design would be the best for us. We then found a builder who agreed to build the lockers and cabinets at a price we could afford. The project was ready to start, but I wanted it to coincide with the completion of the arena. The target date to complete the arena was the first week of November, but the construction crew was doubtful. We held off on the lockers until we had a better idea of when we could take occupancy.

High school hockey in Minnesota begins on the same day for all teams, normally the second Monday in November. As the autumn weeks flew by, it was soon apparent that the target date of an early-November completion for the arena was a bit optimistic. In fact, we weren't able to skate on the new sheet of ice until the end of the first week of December, thereby losing almost four weeks. We were able to book ice only twice a week on the other two sheets in the arena before school. Right out of the starting blocks, we were losing ground fast. We scheduled an away scrimmage for the first day and then another scrimmage at the end of the week. We needed the ice time.

Although it was frustrating at the time, we made the best of the situation by traveling to away scrimmages. Once the building was turned over to the city for occupancy, all the frustrations quickly faded to memories. The lockers and cabinets were installed, and the players moved in. We now had the nicest facility on our side of the metro area.

THE SEASON

I wasn't certain of much when we did begin to skate every day, except that our players were young and inexperienced. More than half the boys could have still been playing bantam hockey, yet here they were scheduled to play against teams with athletes as much as three years older. I also knew we gave away, on average, 40 pounds per player.

After several practices, it was clear that our number one task was skill development. Several of the players hadn't had much coaching in the past, and their skills needed honing. The assistant coaches and I huddled and decided to focus the entire year on fundamental skills, starting with the basics of skating. We weren't concerned about systems or special teams. We knew we'd have trouble winning games unless we raised our skill level.

Our first rude awakening was a preview day in Owatonna with their varsity and the varsity teams from St. Paul Simley and Albert Lea. At these events, teams scrimmage for 45 minutes, rest a bit, and then change opponents to continue scrimmaging. We got hammered in two of those sessions, but we actually survived one with only a two-goal deficit. The boys played hard, but we could not keep up with the older, faster, and stronger players.

In mid-December, we had our first home game against the varsity squad from St. Paul Academy. We lost 2-0 on power-play goals, but we were encouraged. Of greater interest to us was that the school community turned out in force to support the team. The arena was nearly filled to the capacity of 450 spectators, and it sounded like there were thousands. The atmosphere was exciting, and the players suddenly realized that the creation of a new team was something special.

As the weeks rolled by, the team improved and we began to win some games. Winning is good for the soul, especially after a few thrashings. In fact, we started to play so well against several of the teams that they changed their rosters for our second game with them. In the rematch games we found ourselves facing a number of the players from their varsity squads. One school sent their entire varsity team to play us in the second game after we had soundly defeated their JV a couple of weeks earlier. Another school fell behind 3-0 after the fourth shift and promptly shortened their bench for the remainder of the game.

As the season progressed, I was getting a good feel for the different levels of competition with an eye for the next year. I sensed we were already competitive with, or better than, many varsity teams. This was helpful, since I soon had to start scheduling our next season at the varsity level.

When all the games were finished and we totaled the results, we ended up with a regular season record of 12-8-2. This was a much better result than anybody anticipated. More important, we got better individually and as a team. Some players who weren't competitive at the beginning of the year finished very strongly and would keep improving over the next couple of years.

As a team, we made great strides in our relationships between the staff and the players. It takes time for players and coaches to get to know each other and then to trust each other. We accomplished this during the inaugural season, and it was an important stepping stone as we raised the expectations for the following year.

THE OFF-SEASON

The team continued to practice for three weeks after the final game of the season. We used this time to continue working on skills and playing small-area games. The coaches also met with the players individually to help each boy determine what level of commitment he wanted to make in the off-season. Most of the boys played other sports, and we wanted to be careful that we didn't interfere with those seasons. In Minnesota, high school hockey coaches can work with their players only from June 15 until July 31 during the summer. The spring and fall are off limits. We encouraged the boys to play other sports.

For the six weeks of summer that we were permitted to work with our players, we developed a program for our high school team and also for bantams, peewees, and squirts. Many of the summer programs operate four or five times a week, but we thought that was too much. We structured a three-day-a-week program and again encouraged the boys to play lacrosse, soccer, or baseball. Because of the large numbers of youth players in our area, the camps filled easily.

YEAR TWO: BUILD IT AND THEY WILL COME

The more established private school programs in Minnesota have a very strong network of people who encourage players to attend those schools. Direct recruiting of players in high school sports in Minnesota is forbidden. Once a family has officially inquired and requested information from the admissions office, then coaches may contact the prospective student. This is an ongoing activity of most private schools. Financial aid is available based on need, and in some cases tuition is paid by boosters. This has created problems in some of the schools, as athletes are seen as a special class of student and the sports programs begin to dominate the schools. We have elected not to take this path.

Providence Academy will always hold academics as its highest priority. We're lucky because there is a growing interest in private school education. Although we had a short-term need for a few players, families of prospective players began contacting the admissions office shortly after our first season. Once we put our first year behind us, players and their parents began taking a closer look at this unique educational opportunity.

As we enter the 2015-16 seasons, the Providence Academy hockey program has flourished from the humble beginnings. The program has become very competitive in Class A hockey in Minnesota. Some years the team is in the top twenty and some years are a bit leaner due to lower class sizes and the normal ebb and flow of talent. As a school that does not recruit athletes and offers only a need-based tuition assistance program, we are very proud of the accomplishments of our coaches and players. Our players move on to college with a top notch education and they are prepared to be successful in the class room and beyond.

CONCLUSION

Starting a new program at any level takes hard work and patience. I chose to build a program at a high-quality educational institution in a community with an excess of good players. Our program is based on respect, hard work, discipline, and personal responsibility. Our students are expected to excel in the classroom as well as on the ice. We believe that for the right students, we offer an education that will last a lifetime and a hockey experience they will remember forever.

7

Planning and Conducting Productive Practices

Mike Cavanaugh

A few years ago, at the annual convention of the American Hockey Coaches Association, four coaching presentations were scheduled at the same time, with each of the four coaches assigned a topic and placed in a different corner of a large ballroom. Three of the topics—power play, penalty kill, and scoring—attracted sizable crowds of young coaches eager to learn the secrets to success in those areas.

The fourth topic presented by Jerry York, the head coach of Boston College and the all-time wins leader in college hockey, was team building. Coach York looked quite lonely, with only a small group of coaches attending his presentation.

As an assistant to coach York at the time, I had a chance to talk to him about that experience and how few young coaches seemed interested in participating in his talk. It's certainly understandable in today's hockey climate that special teams and scoring goals would be popular topics for coaches at any level. Goals are increasingly hard to come by. Often, certainly at elite levels of play, a game can come down to which club's special teams win out.

Still, in every successful season I've been part of, there's no question that the most important factor in winning is developing a proper team culture. The best time to develop that culture is during daily practices when you interact with your players in an environment you control.

As a qualifier, I'll acknowledge that NCAA Division I hockey is near the top of the competitive pyramid. Therefore, not everything I'll share from my own experience is applicable to youth hockey. We are not only blessed with older, exceptionally skilled players (not to mention state-of-the-art facilities where ice time is ample), but we also have a practice-to-game ratio that youth hockey doesn't enjoy. In fact, we have

Courtesy of UConn Athletic Communications. Photographer: Steve Slade.

it backward in this country, where elite college players have twice as many practices as games while many youth teams have twice as many games as practices.

At the same time, I believe the need to create a true team culture is universal, regardless of the age of the players. My hope is that the practice concepts here will inspire coaches at all levels to assess how they are using the valuable time available to them to develop their players and their team in pursuit of a successful and meaningful experience for all.

VIEWING THE SEASON AS A GAME

At the college level, the season is fairly long. Players take to the ice for captains' practices and supervised skill work in September, and if the team is successful and makes the NCAA tournament, they can play all the way into mid-April. So we break our season into the corresponding elements of a game: warm-up, first period, second period, third period, and overtime.

Our warm-up is September. We are allowed two hours a week during that month, and we use it by scheduling three 40-minute practices each week. Our first period spans the time when games begin in October and runs through the first weekend of December when we break for exams and enjoy a few weeks without games before Christmas.

The second period equates to the months of January and February when our regular season schedule plays out. This is a particularly challenging time. In a game, the second period doesn't have the excitement of the first period or the tension of the third period, but many trophies are won or lost in the middle frame. For us, the second period constitutes the dog days of the season, a time when bad habits can creep in and player focus can start to wander. Players start comparing themselves with others, and they might be struggling with the roles they're being asked to play. Fortunately, the schedule has provided us a good sample size by this point, and we can identify the various roles that players must assume as we approach the tense third period.

The third period is the month of March when we begin postseason play. This encompasses our conference tournament and, if we're successful, the start of the national championship tournament. The tension builds here. At the NCAA Division I level, we deal with a lot of egos; you need big egos to succeed, but they need to be managed. One of my favorite moments is the day the league all-star teams are announced. We can finally say to the players, "Okay, you made it, you didn't. It's over. Now we are just playing for trophies."

As for overtime, that would be the NCAA Frozen Four, and we were very fortunate to get into overtime during many of my years at Boston College. Getting to overtime means you're one of four schools still playing after the Major League Baseball season has begun.

Each of these periods requires a mix of attention to honing individual skills and team systems and also a more specific focus on things that carry a greater priority for that particular time of the season. Sometimes you are where you want to be at that juncture, but more often than not, you feel a need to catch up. We're always trying to get better, no matter where we are in the season.

Conditioning is more of a concern early in the year. As a result, practices are longer earlier in the season. Knowing how long to work can be just as important as knowing what areas need your attention. All along, we're not just working on skills and systems—we're building a team.

TEAM BUILDING THROUGH PRACTICES

You need to preach to your players from day one that you are a team. That has to be stressed in every practice. My favorite part of practice is the meeting beforehand. We have a quote every day, and often one of the players stands up and reads the quote to the team. We reinforce *team* from the first day of practice.

Our season is long, potentially running from September through April. Youth hockey has a long season, too. One universal message we can all deliver is the need to lay down a good foundation and to do it early. If all coaches can preach that it isn't about the individual but about making people around you better, you have a chance to do something special.

No matter what level you coach at, teach kids to be good teammates. Hockey players can be selfish and strive to be noticed. We believe a player can stand out by being a good teammate. As recruiters, we notice guys who work hard. We notice guys who make teammates better. We had a guy who played at Biddeford High School in Maine. He had the attributes we wanted, and although he was playing at a level that might not have been at the top of the pyramid, he showed skills, and he showed that he made his teammates better. That's important to us.

Because of the success Boston College enjoyed under Jerry York while I was there, York was often asked to throw out the first pitch at a Boston Red Sox game. He never put himself in that position. It was always a player, such as the team's captain, or a local Boston kid. It was never about coach York. As coaches, we can send this message often, in so many ways.

How you run your practices is an integral part of the message you want to send. Is it about individual accomplishment or about being part of a team? Is it about getting better alone or helping the people around you get better? If you want your team to be successful, the answer must be the latter, so that collectively a true team emerges with everyone working together to accomplish something as a group, not as individuals.

Figures 7.1 and 7.2 show two sample practices, one from late in our warm-up period of the season and one from our first period.

Following are a few observations about some of the components of a typical practice.

Daily Quote

More often than not, the quote we select reflects a particular message we want to send at that time of the season or even on that particular day. Early in the season, we might be stressing the concept of team. This may become even more appropriate if signs of selfish behavior have started to surface in the locker room or on the ice.

The quote is usually posted early each afternoon. There will be times, most likely early in the season, when we call on a player to get up and address the team. In addition to reading that day's quote, he may have to talk about himself, his family, anything that helps the team get to know him better.

At other times, we might be starting to play undisciplined, taking some bad penalties, so we'll find something topical we can use. Here is a quote from a January practice, during that challenging second period time of year, when we were hurting ourselves with lazy penalties.

> **"The Bruins** gave the Sharks nine power plays, six of them on stick fouls, and San Jose connected on three power play goals in the second period."
>
> *Boston Herald*

This helped us stress what can happen when you take lazy, avoidable penalties. When we get to the third period and overtime, it is all about winning championships. Therefore, the quotes are likely to reflect the immediate challenges at hand, such as this one:

> **"No team** wins the championship holding its breath."
>
> *Harvey Araton, sportswriter*

Points of Emphasis

As coaches, we like to meet every day and talk about our team, our strengths, and our weaknesses. We do the same after a game. Some members of other coaching staffs might be in a hurry to break down video. Conversely, I've always enjoyed going to a restaurant with the other coaches to discuss the game just played.

In most instances, staff members have specific areas of responsibility. One guy has the power play while another has the penalty kill. Maybe one is also responsible for face-offs. I know some staffs where one assistant takes the lead in breaking down the team's needs, while the other coach is responsible for breaking down the next opponent.

Therefore, the points of emphasis in any given practice may result from an overall sense of what should be a priority at that time of the year or, more likely, as the season develops, the result of postgame or prepractice meetings in which we identify what is working and what isn't. The coach who is responsible for a certain area will have the chance to speak up and advocate for a certain drill or time spent on his areas of concern. The final say on all of this typically comes from the head coach, who should welcome input from his staff but remain intimately involved in the design of the practice.

At the youth hockey level, which is quite different from the college game, systems should be the last thing you focus on. The younger the player, the

September 30 practice

Today's quote

"There is no mat space for malcontents or dissenters."
Dan Gable, Olympic wrestler and gold medalist

Points of emphasis

1. Scrum work/battle drills
2. Scrimmage

Practice plan

2:30   Stretch

3:15   Warm-up: 2v0 passing/crease movements

3:25   Shooting drills: Kings full-ice one-touch drill, full-ice
          three-shot drill

3:35   Stretch

3:40   Scrum work/battle drills

3:50   Scrimmage

4:00   Neutral zone 2v2

4:10   Scrimmage

4:20   Scoring game

4:25   Stretch

Notes:

FIGURE 7.1   Sample practice plan from the warm-up period of the season.

October 9 practice

Today's quote

"Once a player thinks he is bigger than the team, you no longer have a team."
Arnold "Red" Auerbach, Boston Celtics

Points of emphasis

1. Penalty killing
2. 3v2 play
3. Neutral zone defense

Practice plan

2:30	Team meeting
2:45	Stretch
3:15	Warm-up/shooting drills
3:30	Penalty-kill series
3:50	Wings 3v2 drill
3:55	Neutral zone defense
4:00	Four-corner 2v1 and 1v1
4:15	Stretch
4:30	Weights

Notes:

FIGURE 7.2 Sample practice plan from the first period time of the season.

more important it is to develop individual skills. Adult coaches can't put their goals and their systems above the team.

Practice Plan

The coaching team places considerable emphasis on those early-season practices. Eight practices into the season, we are doing full-ice clears or defensive zone scrimmaging. We address a number of issues at the start of the season with the idea that we want to be a jack-of-all-trades, not the master of one. We allow plenty of time for practicing individual skills, team systems, and conditioning, the latter more likely emphasized early in the season instead of later.

Here is a snapshot of how we generally plan our days of the week, considering that most weeks we play games on Friday and Saturday nights:

Sunday: We lift weights, do some light skating, and perhaps play 3v3.

Monday: This is our day off. Many teams take Sunday off, but we prefer Monday.

Tuesday: We concentrate on shooting, defense, and penalty killing. This is a long day.

Wednesday: Usually this is our power-play day. It is likely to be a more up-tempo session with odd-man rushes and transition play.

Thursday: This is the day before we play. We might go over some tendencies of our weekend opponent (we often play the same team twice). We finish with 5v6. We also spend considerable time on protecting a one-goal lead, a situation that is quite commonplace.

Much of our practice time focuses on who our opponent is and where the game is being played. Small-ice practices will be scheduled before games in smaller rinks. Conversely, before games against the University of New Hampshire, which has a large, Olympic-size sheet, we might work more on odd-man rushes to simulate the bigger surface.

During my time on the bench, I've become a believer in reinforcing good behaviors. No matter what skill you're working on, reinforce the good things. I hear some coaches say, "Our penalty kill isn't good," or "Our D zone coverage isn't great." To us, it's not about what we are bad at; it's what we can do to get better. We might sit in a coaches' meeting and acknowledge how bad we are at something, but that's not the message we convey to our kids. We point out some neutral zone turnovers, perhaps, and note how we can get better at that. But we will also point out what we did well there. The blunt assessment spoken among coaches is not articulated to the team in the same manner.

We take this same approach when we have a video session. The coaches might look at video and acknowledge our weaknesses, but when we show video to our players, we keep our comments brief and, for the most part, constructive or positive.

TAPERING PRACTICES

Our guys know how to play hockey, so we can shorten practices at different points of the season (e.g., when we are traveling often or near the end of the season). Figures 7.3 and 7.4 show two late-season practice plans, one from the season's third period and one from overtime.

Note how short the practice from the third period is. From warm-up to final stretch, the on-ice activities run just 40 minutes. The last two drills are fun, game-type drills. The only articulated point of emphasis is to be up-tempo. There is value in not practicing—considerable value, actually, especially late in the year. Practices can and should be shorter later in the season, as long as what you do is up-tempo because you can get out of shape quickly.

Western Michigan University coach Andy Murray, who has spent plenty of time behind an NHL bench, will announce that his team will have a 37-minute practice. Not 35 minutes. Not 40 minutes. Instead, he uses an odd number such as 37, and Murray will stick to that time limit exactly. It gets his players' attention, and he has them working hard the entire time.

Also, notice the quote. It's the postseason, and we're now trying to win trophies. So the emphasis is on what it takes to do that.

The sample practice from the overtime period of the season runs 55 minutes. Note the date and the second point of emphasis. This is a practice held during the NCAA's Frozen Four. We are learning a new venue and, as always, staying up-tempo.

March 28 practice

Today's quote

"In every contest, there comes a moment that defines winning from losing. The true warrior understands and seizes that moment by giving an effort so intensive and so intuitive that it could only be called one from the heart."

Pat Riley, former NBA coach

Points of emphasis

1. Up-tempo skate

Practice plan

2:15	Team meeting
2:30	Stretch
3:00	Warm-up
3:10	Shooting drills
3:20	Reasoner 2v1 drill
3:25	Kings 2v1 drill
3:30	Giuliano scoring game/full ice
3:35	Cass showdown/breakaways
3:40	Stretch

Notes:

FIGURE 7.3 Sample practice plan from the third period part of the season.

April 5 practice

Today's quote

"If you play not to lose instead of playing to win, you'll put unnecessary pressure on yourself."

Howard E. Ferguson, editor, *The Edge: The Guide to Fulfilling Dreams, Maximizing Success and Enjoying a Lifetime of Achievement*

Points of emphasis

1. Up-tempo skate
2. Learning the rink

Practice plan

4:15	Team meeting
4:30	Stretch
5:00	Warm-up/shooting drills
5:15	Power play
5:30	Clear 5v2 drill
5:35	Pirates 2v2 drill
5:40	Kings 4v1 drill
5:45	Reasoner 2v1 drill
5:55	Stretch

Notes:

FIGURE 7.4 Sample practice plan from the overtime part of the season.

CONCLUSION

When I first started working on this chapter, I thought the experiences of an NCAA Division I coach might not be as applicable to coaches working at, say, below high school level. But in the end, they are. At all ages, we play a team game, and we are all connected. This can be emphasized by the culture we create at practice, the same culture we want to carry into our games.

8

Skills for Defensemen

Jack Parker

It's quite remarkable how much the game of hockey has changed over the last 20 years. Goals are harder to come by with each passing season. It used to be a race to four; the first team to score four goals in a game would usually win. Now it is a race to three, sometimes two. Gone are the days of the high-flying Edmonton Oilers in the mid-1980s. Good defensemen need to master basic but essential skills in order to be effective.

SKATING BACKWARD

The game would be very difficult for a defenseman if he couldn't skate backward. Most coaches take it for granted that their defensemen can perform this skill. But there is a big difference between skating backward and being able to skate backward well enough to be a good defenseman.

Stay Low

One of the biggest problems for defensemen who have trouble skating backward is they spend too much time moving up and down. A defenseman must try to stay on an even plane as long as he can. The lower he stays, and the less movement he makes upward, the more time and space he will be able to take away from the opposing player. The amount of space he moves upward is the amount of space he could be moving left, right, backward, or forward. He must keep his center of gravity as low as possible for as long as possible. How he stays low is very important. The defenseman doesn't want to bend at the waist and lean forward to stay low, as this will cause him to straighten his legs and lose balance. Instead he should bend at the knees and make sure he keeps his weight over his skates. He wants to be in a position so that his rear end is hanging over his heels. He should look

as though he is about to sit in a chair; to be an efficient backward skater, that's the best position to be in.

Minimize Crossovers

How often have you seen a defenseman trying to pick up speed while skating backward by crossing her feet over again and again? Obviously, when the skater is starting to skate backward, she must cross over to pick up momentum, but once she has picked up some speed, power should be generated by making C-cuts with each skate. When a skater crosses her feet over, her mobility is limited and she is vulnerable to being beaten one on one. If the skater is crossing her feet over while going to her right, she cannot move to her left because all her weight is shifting to the right. The same holds true if she is crossing over to her left. The skater must stay balanced by limiting her crossovers, and she'll be a better backward skater.

One Hand on the Stick

Keeping just one hand on the stick when the other team has the puck will help the defenseman stay low and increase his mobility. The first thing a defenseman does when he puts the second hand (the bottom hand) on the stick is raise his center of gravity. It is just a natural reaction. Instead he should keep the top hand on the stick and keep the stick on the ice in front of his body.

The position of the stick when holding it with one hand is very important. Players have a tendency to place their sticks on the sides of their bodies instead of in front of their bodies. This causes them to lose balance and mobility, two of the most important aspects of being a good backward skater. While keeping one hand on the stick, the defenseman should also remember to limit the movement of his arms. Defensemen have a tendency to swing their arms as they are skating backward. This causes them to lose some of their balance and throws off their center of gravity. Instead, they should keep the upper body as quiet as possible.

GAP CONTROL

No defenseman likes to get beaten one on one. The most embarrassing moment for a defenseman is when a forward skates by him. To compensate for this, defensemen tend to back up into the offensive zone and allow the opposing player time and space with the puck (figure 8.1). All players want time and space to make plays, especially when entering the offensive zone. It is very difficult to be a good defenseman if you don't have good gap control.

Gap control usually starts when a defenseman leaves the offensive blue line. Often when the puck is in the offensive zone, defensemen will stand near the offensive blue line regardless of what is happening in the zone. The blue line is there for one reason and one reason only—offsides. The only time a defenseman should be standing on the offensive blue line is when his team has complete control of the puck. This will allow more space for the forwards when they have the puck as the defenseman becomes an outlet for them.

The blue line does not determine where gap control begins. A defenseman's gap when leaving the offensive zone should be established by how high the opposing forwards are. The longer the play is in the offensive zone, the deeper the opposing forwards tend to be. It is much easier to

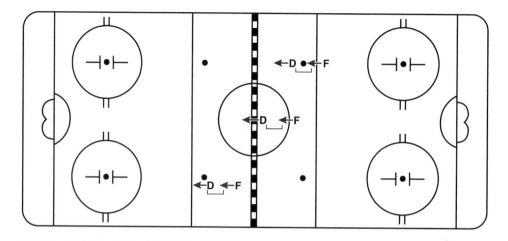

FIGURE 8.1 The defenseman (D) maintains the gap as the forward (F) moves up the ice.

establish a good gap leaving the offensive blue line by using the opposing forwards as a measuring point. By establishing a good gap, the defensemen can slow down the opposing team's transition game. When the defense can slow down the opposition leaving their defensive zone, they allow the defensive team to apply back pressure (back pressure is when the defensive team's forwards are able to pursue the puck carrier from behind; see figure 8.2).

The gap established when leaving the offensive blue line is the gap established through the neutral zone and entering the defensive zone. A

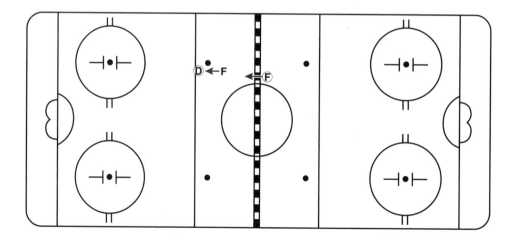

FIGURE 8.2 Forward on the defenseman's team provides back pressure on the opposing forward who has the puck. The defenseman's ability to slow the forward helps his teammate provide pressure from behind.

good gap leaving the offensive blue line allows the defenseman to come through the neutral zone and enter the defensive zone with speed. It is difficult to play a one-on-one attack if the defenseman has to slow down as he enters the defensive zone. While he's slowing down, the opposing forward is usually picking up speed. That is when a defenseman is most susceptible to getting beaten one on one. A good gap allows the defenseman to maintain the same speed as the opposing forward. It also will slow down the forward entering the offensive zone, making him less dangerous. It is difficult for a forward to create offense when a defenseman has established a good gap entering the defensive zone.

Also, if the forward is flying out of the zone, the defenseman might have to get going quickly by first skating forward and then pivoting backward once the proper gap is established. And finally, with regard to vertical gap, the defenseman wants to maintain the good gap from blue line to blue line. This requires that he judge the forward's speed and adjust his own while using good C-cuts, not crossovers.

Sometimes the forward might be skating very fast but in more of a serpentine route. In this situation, his velocity made good (or VMG, a common sailing term) up the ice will not be as fast as it looks. Defensemen must not be fooled. They must judge their opponent's VMG and adjust their speed accordingly.

When talking about gap control, people immediately think of the gap as the space between the forward and the defenseman vertically. What often gets overlooked is the lateral gap. When a defenseman has established a good vertical gap, most forwards will then take the puck to the outside. The mistake most defensemen make is to keep backing up as the forward goes wide. Once the defenseman does this, he loses the advantage he had by establishing a good gap. He's now given the puck-carrying forward time and space to make a play.

Therefore, it is just as important to keep a good lateral gap as it is a vertical gap. The wider the forward goes with the puck, the wider the defenseman should be (figure 8.3). The defenseman should always try to keep his outside shoulder in line with the forward's inside shoulder. This will prevent the forward from cutting back inside and will force him to the outside. There, the defenseman can pivot and take the proper angle at the forward.

Eventually the defenseman will run or angle the forward into the boards. Good gap control by defensemen will cause turnovers inside the defensive blue line and help the defensive team's transition game. Unexpected turnovers are a great way to create offense for a team.

Another way to establish good gap control is following the play up ice. Once the puck is broken out of the defensive zone, the defenseman's

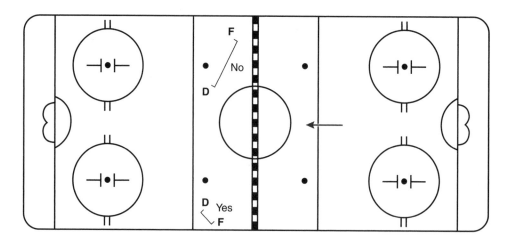

FIGURE 8.3 Maintaining good lateral gap control means the defenseman moves wide with the forward.

responsibilities are to either jump into the play to create an odd-man rush offensively or to follow the play in case a turnover occurs, in which case he needs to create a good gap defensively. The defenseman's job isn't finished once the puck has left the defensive zone. He must always put himself in the best position possible to play defense and establish a good gap. An unexpected turnover in the neutral zone can quickly turn into a scoring chance for the other team. If the puck is turned over in the neutral zone and the defenseman hasn't followed the play up ice, it will be very difficult for a defenseman to establish a good gap because of the amount of space between himself and the forward. The defenseman must always be conscious of creating a good gap. It is one of the most important aspects of playing good defense.

PLAY *THROUGH* PEOPLE, NOT *TO* PEOPLE

Too often defensemen get to the man they're defending and they stop. Instead, when the defenseman gets to the opponent, she must keep skating and stop only when the defenseman has played through the opponent. When a defenseman moves the legs and keeps one hand on the stick and in the proper position, she gives the player being defended less time and space. It will cause the opponent to hesitate and limit the number of plays she can make. If the defenseman moves her feet and keeps her stick on the ice when defending, she'll be surprised by how many passes and shots she can deflect.

USE OF THE STICK

One of the most overlooked skills for defensemen is proper use of the stick. It is such a simple concept that people don't consider it a skill, but it is an essential element of the game. The first thing a defenseman must learn about using his stick properly is to control it with one hand, the top hand (the right hand, if the player is a left-handed shot), as opposed to both hands. When the other team has the puck, a defenseman should have only the top hand on his stick 80 to 90 percent of the time. In addition to aiding backward skating, having one hand on the stick also improves many other aspects of a defenseman's game, including strength, size, mobility, and balance.

When a defenseman is pursuing a forward with the puck, he should have just his top hand on the stick at all times. The first reason is that it makes him bigger. Keeping the top hand on the stick and letting it lead him whenever he chases a forward allows the defenseman to take up extra space. For example, if the stick is four feet long, the defenseman is taking away an extra four feet of ice from the forward if he has one hand on the stick, has the stick blade on the ice, and has the blade aimed at the puck. The defenseman must keep the stick on the ice and let it lead him to the player he is defending.

Stick position is very important. Often defensemen have one hand on the stick but hold the stick sideways across their bodies. Having the stick across the body allows the forward more space. The defenseman must keep the stick in front of his body. He must be conscious of keeping the stick in the shooting or passing lane of the puck. More often than not, a player with the puck will change direction. In this case, the defenseman must have one hand on the stick and must lead with the stick at all times as he changes direction to defend the player with the puck. The most common mistake a defenseman makes when he changes direction is putting his bottom hand on the stick.

Keeping one hand on the stick and keeping the stick on the ice and in front of the body when changing direction will give the defenseman more mobility. One problem defensemen have when they get comfortable playing with one hand on the stick is that they tend to rely on it too much when playing one on one. Defensemen must always remember to play body on body, stick on stick. They must continue to play the body and not be overly conscious of the puck. When the defenseman has one hand on the stick and is defending, he should always remember to move his legs. The stick is just an extension of the body.

A great way to teach players to keep one hand on the stick when defending is to tape a tennis ball to the bottom hand. That way they won't be able to put the bottom hand on the stick when defending people in open ice, and they have to change direction. It is such a natural reaction to put the bottom hand on the stick that many players do not realize how many times they actually do it. Having a tennis ball on the second hand reinforces how often they want to play with two hands on the stick.

There are only two situations in which a defenseman *should* play with two hands on the stick. The first is when he has established body positioning in front of the net, and the second is when he has sealed the opponent along the boards. If the defenseman has established body positioning in front of the net, he should have two hands on the stick so he can gain leverage when battling the opposing player and take away his hands and stick. Tying up someone in front of the net is more about tying up the player's stick and hands than it is about moving the player out from in front of the net. Because players are so much bigger and stronger today, the defenseman's main objective when battling a player in front should be tying up his stick and hands to prevent him from deflecting shots and picking up rebounds.

It's important to have one hand on the stick when a defenseman is pursuing an opposing puck carrier. It is equally important to have two hands on the stick when the defenseman has sealed off the player and he has nowhere else to go. When defending along the boards, the defenseman needs two hands on the stick to battle the opposing player. Having two hands on the stick allows the defenseman to use the boards as leverage. It also gives him a chance to pick up any loose pucks. The defenseman must keep his body between the net and the opposing player. Body positioning is the most important part of any battle along the boards.

BODY POSITION

John Wooden, one of the most successful basketball coaches ever, used to tell his players that two of the keys to being a good basketball player are to "be quick, but don't hurry" and that "you play defense with your feet." These concepts certainly apply to being a good defenseman in hockey. Earlier in the chapter, I discussed taking away time and space while defending. What often happens to a defenseman when he is pursuing a puck carrier is that he goes to the player out of control, trying to take away as much time and space as possible. He is so anxious to play through his man that he forgets the importance of body positioning. Defenders must go through a thought process. The first objective for the defender is to keep his body between the net and the offensive player. His second objective is to get to his man as quickly as possible (but under control), taking away time and space, but not at the expense of being beaten one on one and allowing the opponent to get between himself and the net.

How often have you seen a defenseman defend a forward with the puck along the boards, but he gets beaten because he defended so aggressively that when he hit the forward, he lost his balance and fell to the side of the opposing player? It is a mistake. The defenseman has worked hard to gain a defensive advantage by having his body between the net and the offensive player. He needs to keep that advantage. Most offensive chances are created because the defenseman loses his main objective of body positioning (remember: "You play defense with your feet").

The longer a defenseman battles an opposing player along the boards, the harder it is to maintain body positioning. When this happens, the defenseman should use the forward as leverage and push off him to recover his own body positioning. This will create some space between the defenseman and the opposing forward and allow the defenseman to attack again. By pushing off the opposing forward along the boards, the defenseman puts himself closer to the net while also pushing the opponent farther from it. A defenseman rarely will get beaten one on one if he keeps moving his feet and is constantly aware of keeping his body between the net and the offensive player.

Another important aspect of successfully defending a one-on-one attack is protecting the Grade A area. The Grade A area (figure 8.4) is the space between the two circles in the defensive zone (sometimes referred to as "the house"). When protecting this area, the defenseman must establish good body position, with his body between the net and the offensive player, and then beat the opponent he is responsible for to the point of contact.

For example, when an opposing defenseman has the puck on the blue line, he must establish good body position first and then initiate contact

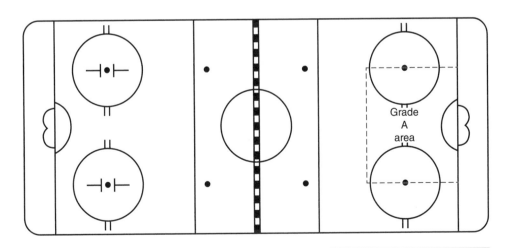

FIGURE 8.4   Grade A area.

with the man he is responsible for. It is hard to defend in front of the net if the defenseman isn't going to his man. Waiting for the opponent to come to him puts the defenseman at a disadvantage, because the opponent will be the one dictating the contact. If the defenseman initiates the contact, he can engage the opponent outside the Grade A area, and the opponent will be less of a threat to tip a shot or pick up a rebound. The defenseman always wants to engage his responsibility outside the Grade A area. This also holds true when covering during face-offs. The defenseman must make sure he is the one initiating the contact as the puck is being dropped.

BREAKING OUT OF THE DEFENSIVE ZONE

The most difficult skill a defenseman must develop is the ability to break the puck out of the defensive zone. Unfortunately, dumping the puck into the offensive zone has become an offensive tactic for many teams. Forwards know how hard it is for a defenseman to turn and get a puck that has been dumped in. To successfully break the puck out of the zone, the defenseman must know what she is going to do with the puck before she gets to it. While skating to pick up a puck in the defensive zone, the defenseman looks over her shoulder (shoulder checking) to gauge how close the forechecker is. This will also let her know where her teammates are for passing options.

This isn't easy. Most defensemen want to get to the puck as quickly as possible and often forget to shoulder check while skating to a loose puck in the defensive zone. The defenseman who is not skating to pick up the puck must still let her partner know what's going on by talking to her. At the same time, she should be putting herself in the best position to be a passing outlet for her partner. Often, the defenseman who isn't picking up the puck thinks she has no responsibilities. That's a mistake. She has a responsibility every second she is on the ice.

The next thing defensemen must remember is to always move the feet while shoulder checking. The defenseman wants to separate herself from the forechecker so she'll have more time when she gets to the puck. This will allow her to make better decisions. The defenseman also needs to take a good angle to the puck so she has options to handle or pass it once she gets the puck on her stick. Defensemen must always remember to take pride in puck possession.

Sometimes the defenseman will do everything right when going to pick up a puck in the defensive zone, but when she gets to it the forechecker is right on her. The defenseman shouldn't just get rid of the puck for the sake of getting rid of it. Sometimes the best play is no play. The defenseman must not pass her problems to somebody else. Nothing is wrong with keeping the puck in the area where it was dumped and protecting it. This will limit the number of turnovers, which limits scoring chances for the opponent.

Many scoring chances are created when a defenseman gets to a puck that was dumped into the defensive zone, feels the forechecker on her, and then gets rid of the puck without knowing which team will receive it. The defenseman should always have a purpose, either to pass the puck to a teammate or to get it to the next zone where one of her team's forwards can gain possession.

A defenseman who has retrieved a dumped puck and is being pursued by a forechecker has several options to shed the forechecker, giving herself more time with the puck. Breaking the puck out of her own end becomes much easier if she can lose the first forechecker. Once she loses the first forechecker, the opposing team can establish a forecheck only if another forward leaves the player she's responsible for and tries to pressure the defenseman with the puck. This gives the defenseman another passing option.

There are two great ways to lose the first forechecker. First, the defenseman can use the net to her advantage. Second, she can escape with a tight turn in the opposite direction. Using the net properly will make it very tough for the forechecker to cause a turnover. The first thing the defenseman must do is to make sure the forechecker can't get between her and the net. The defenseman wants to keep the forechecker on the outside so that when she gets to the net, the defenseman is taking an angle that allows her to skate as close to the net as possible. Once she has established inside positioning, the defenseman must continue to keep the forechecker on the outside of her body. This will prevent the forechecker from getting between her and the net.

If by chance the forechecker has done a good job of getting inside the defenseman before she gets to the net, then using a tight escape turn is the best way to lose the forechecker. The only way this turn will work is if the defenseman with the puck sells the fact that she is trying to get to the net. Moving her feet at all times while skating toward the net will force the forechecker to overcommit, which will allow the defenseman to make a tight turn away from the net and lose the forechecker. Once she's changed direction, the defenseman must keep her feet moving and push the puck up ice to create distance between herself and the forechecker. The more she can make decisions while moving her feet, the more success she will have breaking the puck out of the defensive zone.

Another great way to lose the forechecker is to use a partner as an outlet. The defenseman skates toward the net and lets the forechecker come to her. If the defenseman's partner is out in front of their net as the defenseman and forechecker approach the net, the defenseman can bank the puck off the boards in the opposite direction that she and the forechecker are skating. Her partner can cross the goal line and pick up the puck and skate it out.

Another option is for the defenseman to bring the forechecker to her before she gets near the net and then pass the puck behind the net to her partner in the other corner. I like to refer to the defenseman who doesn't have the puck as the breakout D because if the defenseman with the puck can find the breakout D, she can break out of the zone easily.

ODD-MAN RUSHES

At times, a single defenseman must defend against two opponents (a two-on-one situation) or two defensemen must defend against three opponents (a three-on-two situation).

The two on one is really a two on two when you factor in the goaltender. The goalie takes the shooter and the defenseman plays the middle, making a pass difficult but not allowing the puck carrier to complete a breakaway untouched.

CONCLUSION

Defensemen are responsible for protecting the net, blocking the passing lanes, and upsetting the momentum of the offense during breakaways. A good defenseman has mastered the key physical skills of backward skating and proper stickhandling. He understands gap control, both horizontal and vertical. He knows how to play the opponent aggressively without overcommitting and giving the opponent a chance to get past him. When he defends successfully and gains control of the puck, he knows how to begin an offensive play by losing the forechecker and sending the puck to a teammate who can control it toward the opponent's net. He doesn't panic when he's outnumbered near the net, but maintains focus and works with his goalie to keep the opponent from scoring. A good defenseman is the cornerstone of a successful team.

9

Skills for Forwards

Rick Comley

Our early years in hockey are the fun years, when five- to eight-year-olds chase the puck, fall down, and get back up again. Everyone is praised, and the thrill is found in simply playing the game. Like all sports, hockey evolves quickly into skill development and team play, and the chase to move up the ladder begins.

This chapter breaks down the areas of the game a player must master to some degree to be a better forward. The better players are at these skills, the farther up the ladder they will go.

With that in mind, understand that coaches search high and low for smart, skilled players who are hard workers. The better the skills, the more options the player has. This chapter covers three categories: individual skills, mental skills, and team play skills.

INDIVIDUAL SKILLS

Although hockey is first and foremost a team sport, the best teams are full of players with excellent individual skills.

Skating

Every coach is looking for forwards who are great skaters, players who are strong on their feet and have long, powerful strides; excellent balance; good lateral movement; and great quickness over the first five steps. These players are ideal. But in the end, most players don't have all these qualities. The ultimate measuring device, therefore, is whether they get to where they need to be at the right time.

Areas of skating that must be developed include the following:

- Powerful stride: Long and smooth strides generate speed without creating fatigue.

Courtesy of MSU Athletic Communications.

- ◆ Wide base: A wide base provides the strength and balance to play in traffic and win battles.
- ◆ Quick five steps: Those first five steps are necessary to create separation from the opponent, which ultimately leads to scoring chances.
- ◆ Edge control: Players must master using the inside and outside edges. The best skaters use limited ice and turn without losing time.
- ◆ Pace: The smart forward moves at the same pace as the play, staying within striking distance of the puck to support or be a passing option. Too many players skate all out only when they have the puck or they're sure they can be the primary passing option. Too many offensive and defensive opportunities are lost because of poor pace.

Players must work to develop fast- and slow-twitch muscle fibers to increase their quickness and endurance and to increase the amount of time they can play at full speed. Too many players hit the wall after 15 to 20 seconds of maximum exertion and have to leave the ice. Short recovery time is another key trait, since the player who can go all out and recover quickly for the next shift is very valuable to a coach.

All these areas can be developed and improved and must be worked on continually. The key is that the coach must be creative when working on skating development, so the players don't always view it as conditioning or punishment.

Passing and Receiving

Hockey is the fastest team sport there is, and nothing creates speed like good puck movement—and nothing creates more ragged play than sloppy puck movement. One point players should always keep in mind is that the player receiving a pass must come to the puck and present a good target for his teammate.

Forehand Passing

Players must be able to make hard passes with a snap or slide action, right to the blade of the receiving player's stick. Good passers can see the ice well, anticipate the speed of the player they're passing to, and pass through traffic when needed. At times a saucer, or elevated, pass is required to get the puck over an opponent's stick to a teammate.

A critical skill is the timing of the pass. Instead of giving the puck up as soon as possible, too many players wait too long before making a pass to give the receiver time to figure out what to do next. Good players already know what to do with the puck before receiving it.

Backhand Passing

This is a more difficult pass that requires wrist and arm action to cover any distance. Most players keep their top hand too tight to the body rather than letting it freely move in front of the body. Hands should be approximately 12 to 14 inches apart. The puck starts off the back foot and is pulled forward before being released off the front foot in the manner needed. Soft hands and good wrist action are hallmarks of good passers.

Players should receive the puck in front of the forward foot and let the puck settle off the back foot in a passing or shooting position. This is called cushioning the puck, and it lets the player control a hard pass and be ready to do something with the puck. The same technique is used for

---

Selecting a Stick

We're in the era of one-piece composite sticks that shoot bullets but break easily, cost a considerable amount of money, and make receiving the puck difficult. Players must experiment until they find a stick that suits them and allows them to execute all required puck skills. The stick must be durable enough to withstand the slashing and force put into each shot, and it must give the player the right level of confidence not to pass up shooting opportunities.

---

forehand and backhand passes. The better passing and receiving skills a team has, the faster the team can play the game.

Shooting and Scoring

The four different types of shots used by players are the wrist shot, snap shot, slap shot, and backhand shot.

The wrist shot is much like passing action. The puck starts off the back foot and is drawn forward and usually released off the front foot. The wrists roll over or under to control the height of the shot. It takes longer to release the puck this way, and for this reason the wrist shot tends to disappear from the game at higher levels of play.

The snap shot is the most popular shot of college, junior, and pro players. Snapping the wrist results in a quick release off either foot. A goaltender has a more difficult time knowing when this shot is coming and where it is going. Players can be off balance when shooting. This shot is used from 20 feet or less and is usually aimed at the upper part of the net.

The slap shot is the hardest shot but takes the longest time to get away unless the player is shooting off a pass or one-timing the puck. This skill is very effective but difficult to do. The slap shot is a disappearing skill as most teams play solid defense and don't give players on the rush enough time to get this shot away. A one-timer is used mostly on superior-man rushes and on the power play. If executed properly, this shot poses a great deal of difficulty for the goalie.

Unfortunately, the backhand shot is a disappearing art. Goaltenders hate backhand shots, primarily because they are unpredictable and difficult to track. The biggest problem with this type of shot is the time it takes to develop an effective backhand and the time it takes to release the puck.

All four of these shots require proper skill and technique. Good knee bend, effective weight transfer, and dynamic wrist action are needed for the release and timing to propel the puck with enough velocity to score.

The most difficult aspect of the game today is scoring. Coaches are constantly on the lookout for players who have a track record of producing from level to level. It's very difficult to teach scoring, in part because it involves so many elements, including skill, confidence, and vision.

Scorers get multiple chances per game. They know where to go and when to get there. They have an ability to see what the goaltender is doing and can anticipate his reaction to their scoring opportunities. They know when to shoot, what type of shot to use, and where to put the puck, and they have the patience to execute.

Plus, everyone blocks shots these days. Players must keep their heads up when they shoot to increase their chances of getting their shots through traffic.

Most of today's goaltenders are butterfly style, so traditional scoring areas are somewhat different from the past. When goalies remained on their feet more, the best scoring locations were the four corners and through the goalie's legs (figure 9.1). Now that goalies drop more often and stay down, areas just above their pads and just inside the posts (1 and 2; figure 9.2) are the best targets. A high shot next to the goalie's head (3 and 4) can be effective. All four of these areas are tough for goalies to reach with their hands. The 5 hole remains a good target.

Driving to the Net

Another diminishing skill is driving to the net. This requires keeping the puck away from the defender, putting an arm or leg out to keep the opponent's stick from getting to the puck, and being strong enough to fight

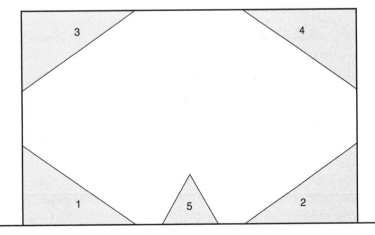

FIGURE 9.1 Past scoring locations: the four corners and through the goalie's legs.

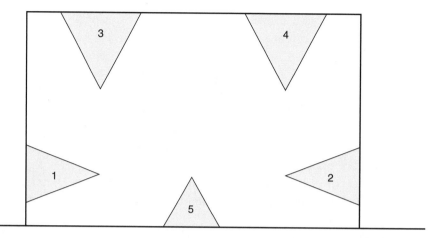

FIGURE 9.2 Current scoring areas: above the pads and inside the posts, next to the goalie's head, and through the goalie's legs.

through resistance. Most players drive better to the net on their backhand side than they do on their shooting side.

MENTAL SKILLS

Don't be misled by the brevity of this middle section. Its meaning and effect on an athlete's season and a team's success are almost impossible to overstate.

Confidence

Every good player must have confidence to be successful. Confidence is difficult to gain and easy to lose. Every coach must work constantly to build confidence by putting players in positions in which they can be successful, which in turns helps increase confidence levels.

The challenge for coaches and players alike is preventing confidence loss, which happens when a player isn't having success and the coach replaces him in situations when the player thinks he should be on the ice. A good teaching tool for players and coaches is to use video of successful situations from the past. The only way for a player to regain confidence is to trust himself, be patient, and work harder.

Every season presents many challenges, highs, and lows for each player. Forwards come under scrutiny every game because so much public perception regarding how good they are is directly related to scoring and producing points. Not all forwards are scorers or are expected to score, but they are judged in some way, if not by points, then by categories such as hits or plus–minus. Today, everyone is expected to contribute offensively.

Attitude

A critical component of every good team is that the players have a positive, team-first attitude, and they share the joy and excitement of team success over individual accolades. This is a trait that all coaches want in their players, especially their best players.

If your best players have the best attitudes on the team, then your team's chances of being successful increase dramatically. Proper attitude can include flexibility (as to where you play and whom you play with), adaptability (as to when or how much you play), and work capacity. The more diverse you are, the better you are.

TEAM PLAY SKILLS

A proper attitude can help athletes develop other essential skills for the game, including team play skills. A single athlete does not make a winning team, hence the importance of developing strong team play skills such as the following.

Puck Protection and Cycling

Two offensive concepts that are critically important in today's game are puck protection and cycling. Both allow teams to keep the puck for extended periods of time and help to establish control of the game and create scoring chances. For puck protection, players must keep their bodies between the puck and the defender. This skill that forwards use mostly in the offensive zone can draw penalties from an impatient defender and lead to scoring chances. Players who are good at puck protection usually are strong, have excellent balance, and aren't afraid to play in traffic.

Cycling involves two or three forwards at the offensive goal line and causes nightmares for defenders. In the basic concept, the first player cycles or skates up or down the boards and bumps or chips the puck to a new area while protecting the puck from an opponent (figure 9.3). The second forward retrieves the puck and can continue to cycle, spin back (figure 9.4), or bump the puck to a new corner.

Some teams prefer the safety of a two-man cycle with a third forward in a defensive position, while other teams use all three forwards in an aggressive cycle to generate scoring chances. Ideally, you always have a

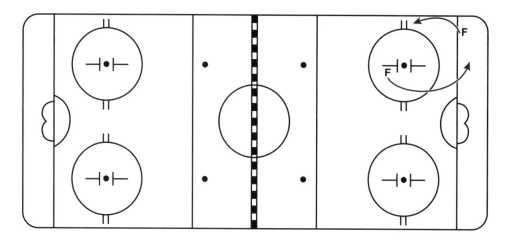

FIGURE 9.3 Cycle up.

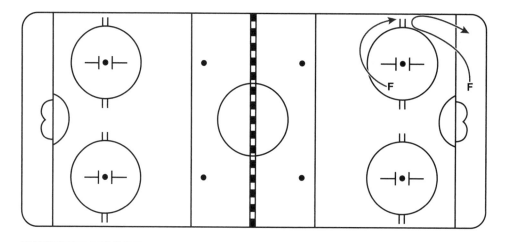

FIGURE 9.4 Spin back.

player in a good scoring position to receive a pass or play a rebound on a successful cycle.

Depending on how much of an advocate of cycling you are, you can begin to add moving screens and picks that don't create enough interference for referees to call the penalty. Teams that master legal picking and screening can create more scoring chances.

An unfortunate spin-off from puck protection and cycling is players turning their backs to defenders, leading to too many hits from behind and dangerous contact situations. It's an issue every coach should be aware of.

Contact

Fans have always loved speed, scoring, and contact and always will. Hitting is disappearing from the game, especially big hits, but contact will always be part of hockey.

The basic rules say a player can hit when the opponent is not in a vulnerable position, the player doesn't take more than three steps, and the player keeps the stick and elbows down. In today's game, contact to the head and big hits into the boards are automatic calls. Big open-ice hits are rare but still allowed under the rules.

Angling

Angling is an old concept being rediscovered. A player pursues the puck carrier in order to angle her to a position in which the pursuer has the advantage, to prevent the puck carrier from moving the puck up the ice, and to force a pass. The end result is to rub the puck carrier off into the boards or mirror her as she attempts to join the play. This is particularly necessary in girls' and women's hockey, where checking is forbidden. The women's game still bans checking but prominently features angling the player off the puck. Even without checking, women's hockey has become more physical as the speed and skill of the players have improved.

Playing Without the Puck

Players spend probably 90 percent of their time on the ice without the puck. Therefore, they must have an excellent understanding of what to do in all situations and areas of the ice. A key concept in today's game is back pressure on the puck, taking away time and space from the puck carrier.

Even forwards must play defense. Backchecking refers to covering an opponent who doesn't have the puck without hooking, holding, or interfering. The forward must match the skating speed of the opponent, stay within a stick length, and stay inside and between the forward's net and the opponent. The forward must also be aware of where the puck is and whether the opponent he is defending is a passing option.

There is an emphasis on eliminating interference, hooking, and holding from the game, which requires backcheckers to work harder (i.e., keep the legs moving and not just reach with the stick). Players must be completely aware of what is happening around them.

Communication

This skill should be so simple, but it is *so* difficult to get teams to do, and it frustrates coaches at every level. The players who communicate the best are, not surprisingly, in the National Hockey League.

Teach players to communicate when they want a teammate to pass or to shoot. Make sure everyone uses the same commands. Defensive confusion can be eliminated by talking and communicating. Too many times, opportunities for scoring chances are wasted because players don't communicate. Remember that talk can trigger action.

Blocking Shots

Forwards who are willing to block shots provide a key defensive skill that can help prevent goals. The ideal method is a one-knee block, which allows the forward to block and recover and to react to a fake shot. Some players prefer dropping to two knees or sliding with both legs in front of the puck. The last two techniques are all-or-nothing attempts and can leave the player vulnerable to being faked out or stepped around.

Defensive Play

Forwards must play defense in all three zones of the ice. In the offensive zone, the general rule is to always have a high forward in a position to backcheck so that every attack situation is an even-up rush.

In the neutral zone, forwards must again be on the defensive side of attackers and must read and react to puck movement. Most coaches use a version of a 1-2-2 or a 1-4. This requires the center to steer the puck into one winger, while a second winger takes away the opposing center or protects the weak side.

The primary system in the defensive zone is three-on-three low, and wingers cover the puck-side defense and the slot. It essentially requires man-on-man play, with all five players ready to release and help in dangerous scoring situations. The center should be second into the corner and come in to get the puck, not play physically. Again, recent teaching has progressed to five men plugging up the front of the net and filling shooting lanes. No one turns and boxes out anymore.

Special Team Play: Penalty Killing and Power Play

Here are the traits you should look for in a good penalty killer:

- ◆ Able to stop and start quickly
- ◆ Able to read options and anticipate

- Has an active stick
- Willing to block shots
- Competitive and strong enough to win battles and clear the puck
- Able to win face-offs

For the power play, you want forwards who can do the following:

- Play smart and see the ice
- Pass and receive passes
- Shoot off the pass
- Score
- Compete in traffic
- Recognize two-on-one opportunities
- Play unselfishly
- Keep from panicking

Both the penalty kill and power play are critical to team success. Teams should strive to score during power plays 15 to 22 percent of the time and kill penalties 87 to 90 percent of the time. A team with a special team index (combined power play percentage and penalty killing percentage) of 107 to 110 likely will win more games than it loses.

CONCLUSION

Hockey is a great game, played at high speed with tremendous intensity. I've attempted to note the multiple skills a forward must possess or develop, as well as the diverse situations in which forwards are involved over the course of each game. The willingness to understand the game and improve one's skills is essential to the team's success and a player's continued improvement.

Mastering the entire process of individual skill development, mental awareness, and involvement in team play situations is what turns an average forward into an impact forward. These actions lead to team success first and individual success second.

10

Skills for Goaltenders

Joe Bertagna

The position of goaltending and the availability of instruction have changed dramatically over the past few decades. As the game of hockey has changed, goaltenders have adapted and aided greatly by improvements in the quality and size of equipment. More books, videos, DVDs, and goaltending schools are available than ever before. As a result, better athletes have been attracted to the position. Here is a look at some of the skills today's goaltenders need to master to be successful.

BALANCED BASIC STANCE

As with any athletic position, a goaltender must establish a good foundation. That means assuming a balanced basic stance (figure 10.1). A goaltender will actually employ two or three different types of stances during a game depending on the situation. The basic stance that most coaches refer to allows the goaltender to feel comfortable and balanced. It's a stance from which he can initiate all movements, whether reacting to shots (making saves) or moving the entire body from one spot to another.

Another purpose of the basic stance is simply to fill the net. Gloves, for example, should cover open space rather than be positioned directly in front of the body. The catch glove should be open and facing the shooter, not only to snare the puck but also because an open glove covers more net than a closed glove.

Here is a checklist for establishing a proper and balanced basic stance:

- Skates approximately shoulder-width apart or slightly wider
- Weight on balls of the feet, slightly pushing on inside edges of skate blades
- Knees bent, chest up, so the weight of the shoulders isn't out ahead of the knees

FIGURE 10.1 The basic stance from *(a)* the front and *(b)* the side.

- Stick blade flat on ice, covering the area between the skates
- Stick blade four to six inches ahead of the skates to cushion shots along the ice
- Gloves held at roughly the same height, usually just above the knee, about midthigh
- Elbows tight to the body, to eliminate interior holes, and hands slightly forward so the goalie can see them

Regarding the last point, if a goalie looks straight ahead and can't see his hands peripherally, they're too close to the body. When a puck is shot high, the goalie wants to see the puck all the way into his glove or body, and this is better accomplished when he has his gloves in sight from the start.

There are at least two other variations of the basic stance. When a puck is so close that the goalie realistically can't react to a shot, the pads come together tightly and the catch arm drops alongside the pad, glove open and tight to the pad. In effect, the goalie is building a solid wall to defend against a shot. This stance is also employed against poor angles, such as when a player walks out of the corner along the goal line.

Another stance variation comes just before a shot, when goalies who prefer to drop into a butterfly (figure 10.2) allow their skates to shift wider than shoulder width. This facilitates the butterfly drop but can also be dangerous if the opposing player doesn't shoot. If that player passes the puck or moves with it, the goalie, who has spread out too much, will have difficulty regrouping and moving his body, particularly if he must move laterally.

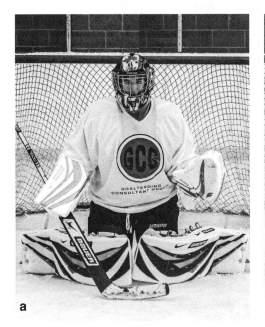

a b

FIGURE 10.2 Butterfly position from *(a)* the front and *(b)* the back.

RECOVERY TO STANCE

All goalies are taken out of position during a game, and the ability to recover to their feet back to a proper stance is critical. A goaltender who is out of position should first locate the puck, even before getting up, and then position the stick. A shot may come the goalie's way before he fully recovers, so getting the stick in place to make a save is vital. At this point, the goalie can get up, or recover, behind the stick.

Some young goalies find it helpful to make getting to their knees a preliminary goal. This halfway station makes the chore of recovering less daunting. When recovering from the knees, the goalie must keep his stick on the ice and get up behind his stick. Younger goalies will get up one leg at a time. Eventually, they will learn to hop up with both legs at once.

When recovering from the stomach, the goalie will slide to his knees and then get up the same way as when recovering from the knees.

Recovering from the back causes huge problems for younger goalies, who often spin around in a 180-degree turn, taking their eyes off the puck. Goalies should never turn their back to the puck in recovering (to their knees or to their feet). Goalies should push down on the catch glove as they raise their heads. This allows them to locate the puck before getting to their knees and placing the stick on the ice. They then recover behind the stick.

When a goalie is on his side, he should bend his bottom leg at the knee and bring the top leg over. Again, the goalie gets to his knees before completing the recovery.

GOALTENDER SKATING

It is a common cliche, and not altogether accurate, that the goalie must be the best skater on the team. It is a rare team in which the goalie *is* the best skater, but this old adage is actually meant to dispel the opposite idea, which is that because a goalie doesn't skate far or often, he can get away with being a weak skater.

Goalies wear 25-plus pounds of extra equipment and must move quickly from spot to spot, down and up, and side to side. Good goaltending requires proficiency in a *different type* of skating to move efficiently with all that extra gear. Failure to do so can cost a team dearly.

Goalie skating—and there are a number of specific techniques—requires the goaltender to move while maintaining the basic stance described earlier. The goalie can't always expect to be set when a shot comes, so she must move in a manner that allows her to execute a save technique even while moving.

The basic types of goalie skating are forward and back, the shuffle, and the T-glide or drop step. In forward and back, the front (or face) of the pads always face the puck. The goalie moves with small C-cuts by pushing off the inside edges, alternating one skate and then the other. The stick must stay on the ice, hands are out, and the chest is up. The goalie must be careful to maintain balance and not let the shoulders get ahead of her knees.

The shuffle (figure 10.3) is a series of small lateral steps. The goalie opens the lead pad, then snaps the back pad together. The skate blades always point out straight, facing the puck. This allows the goalie to stay in her stance against a puck carrier who is cutting across the front of the goal.

The T-glide (figure 10.4) is named because in midmove the skate blades nearly form a T. The drop step (figure 10.5) is similar. These techniques are used in reaction to a free-moving puck farther from the net. The lead skate turns and points in the direction the goalie wants to move, and the back skate pushes off the inside edge to propel the goalie. The goalie should lead with the hands and stick.

Rarely do goalies sprint or do crossovers. There are three times when speed is needed: when a goalies takes a few quick steps to play a loose puck, when a goalie goes to the bench during a delayed penalty on the other team, and when a goalie is pulled for an extra attacker at the end of the game. As for crossovers, the only crossover step done with any regularity is the first step when going behind the net to stop a puck that has been dumped into the zone (older goalies).

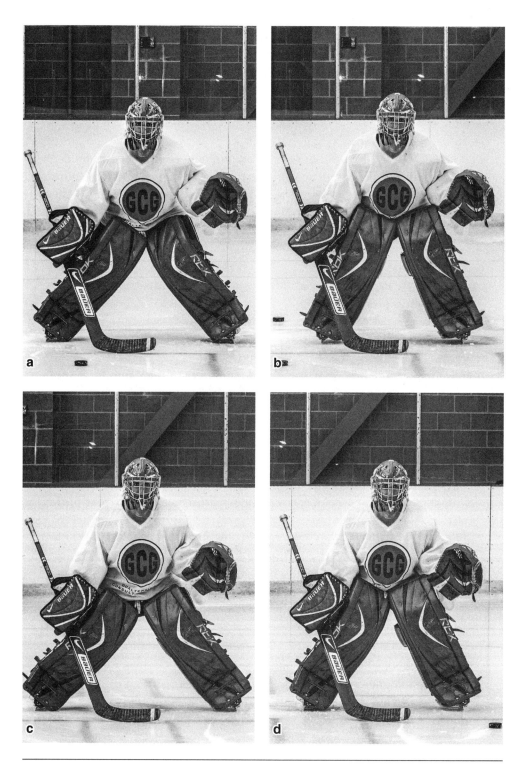

FIGURE 10.3 The shuffle step.

FIGURE 10.4 The T-glide.

FIGURE 10.5 The drop step.

POSITIONING SKILLS (PLAYING ANGLES)

A goalie who makes 30 saves in a game spends about 30 seconds in the act of making saves. The rest of the time is spent preparing for action. The goalie must constantly work to find the puck and get in proper position so that the eventual save is most efficient. Being in the right place at the right time is the key to successful goaltending. This is also known as positioning, or playing the angles.

The first lesson in learning positioning is understanding shooter angles. An angle is formed by running imaginary lines from the puck to each goalpost. If you add the goal line, you can visualize a triangle.

While the size of the open goal is always four feet by six feet, the space available to the shooter changes as puck position changes. The widest angle, or biggest opening, is directly in front of the goal. The angle gets narrower as the puck moves from in front toward the corners.

The goalie has three basic responsibilities for playing angles properly:

1. The goalie must be centered in the middle of the angle. Another imaginary line runs from the puck through the center of the goalie to the center of the goal line, between the posts. It is important to remind goalies to line up on the puck rather than the shooter's body.

2. The goalie must have depth. The goalie should move out to fill the angle, or at least leave minimal space to either side. When the puck is directly in front, the angle is wider, so the goalie must move out farther. When the puck is deeper in the zone, the angle is narrower, and sometimes the goalie doesn't need to move out at all.

3. The goalie must be squared to the puck. The best way for goalies to grasp this is to ask them to imagine a large spotlight on their chest. They must turn their body so that the spotlight shines on the puck wherever it is. If they do that, their shoulders and hips will be the same distance from the puck in most shooting scenarios (unless the puck is close to the goal line).

Older goalies need to take into account another set of skills related to angles. Situational positioning introduces the effect of specific situations, particularly in determining depth. If a puck carrier has options—he can pass to people, he can shoot, or he can keep coming—the goalie must stay home and not move out too far. The different ways the puck might be moved could cause problems for a goalie who has strayed too far from the goal. If, however, the puck carrier, or more specifically a shot on goal, is the only real immediate threat, the goalie can move out more aggressively to defend against the shot.

It should be noted that contemporary goalie coaches place less emphasis on moving out aggressively. This is partly an acknowledgement of how quick the game is and that a goalie who comes out too far might not be able to get back in time. It is also a direct effect of larger goalie equipment. Goalies now fill as much net while positioned on the goal line as previous generations did three steps out. The current movement aimed at shrinking the size of goalie equipment could result in a reexamination of positioning, with goalies needing to come out another step in certain situations. The limits for the size of gloves and leg pads have been reduced, but those changes have not had an appreciable effect on style of play. In fact, some goalies report that the smaller pads make them more agile. Until rule makers find a way to reduce the size of upper-body equipment (chest and arm protectors), current changes aren't expected to make much difference.

PUCK-STOPPING SKILLS

Every scoring opportunity has three parts to it: what happens before the shot, what happens the moment the puck is released toward the goal, and what happens after the initial action.

Before the Shot

Before the shot, the goalie has to be set in a proper stance, in the right place, and aware of everything that is happening in the area (who might deflect a shot, who might get a rebound, where helpful teammates are, and so on).

At Moment of Release

When the puck is released, the goalie must be able to execute any number of save techniques efficiently. All moves begin from the balanced stance discussed earlier. Often, one side of the body initiates a move and the other makes the save. For example, a puck heading low to the goalie's left side will likely be stopped by a piece of equipment on that side: a pad, a glove, or the stick moving in that direction. But the movement will likely be initiated by the right skate pushing off its inside edge and moving the body to the left.

The goalie's eyes should follow the puck directly into the piece of equipment that is stopping the puck and, equally important, follow the puck where it goes afterward, in case there's a second shot.

The goalie must move efficiently. That is, the goalie should move only what must move, where it must move. Large, dramatic moves are often unnecessary and even counterproductive because they can leave a goalie out of position for a rebound. Everything should move in harmony toward the puck. Make sure the body isn't fighting itself. For example, on a shot low to the left, a goalie sometimes moves his left pad and lower body left toward the puck, while his head and upper body lean back to the right. This is not an efficient move. Everything must move left toward the puck.

After the Initial Action

The after part of a scoring opportunity involves recovering to the stance, perhaps tying up or clearing loose pucks, or maybe even facing a second shot (a rebound).

Goalies should stop shots along the ice with the stick, backed up by the pads or skates. Long ago, they were taught to make actual skate saves, but that doesn't happen today. Encourage your goalies to stay on their feet whenever possible, stopping the puck by moving the stick along the ice, backed up by skates. When the shot is on the corner or comes through traffic, the goalie can back up the stick with a full pad dropped flush to the ice. Sticks can direct pucks with more precision than pads alone. Just dropping and allowing the puck to hit the pads often leads to dangerous rebounds out front.

High shots can be caught or trapped against the body. Shots high to the stick side can be deflected away by turning the blocker at the moment of impact. Goalies must take care to avoid directing those shots out front or to opposing players.

Shots directly at the goalie often cause more problems than those to the sides. Many goalies freeze and let those shots deflect off the body. On-ice shots should be cushioned by the stick as they are stopped, then cleared or tied up. Higher shots may be trapped against the body if not caught or deflected cleanly.

Deflected shots and shots through screens can be dangerous and tricky, but they are not unstoppable. Goalies must play swivel-headed, looking for potential deflectors in the area. When a shot is sent toward a potential deflector, the goalie must move, either upright or down, and be centered on the stick causing the deflection. The goalie should move as close to the point of deflection as possible, just as he should move out on screens. The purpose of this aggressive positioning is to limit direct lines from puck to open net.

PLAYING A BREAKAWAY

Goalies must develop strategies for certain situations that come up regularly. A clean break by an opposing player, or a breakaway, is something goalies don't want to see, but they are common. Increasingly, different levels of play are employing breakaways to decide tie games in various shootout formats.

Here is an example of how a goalie thinks in developing a strategy for stopping breakaways. This was first prepared in 2004 for *USA Hockey Magazine*. Goalies are best served by having a method. In this instance, having a method means the goalie knows what he would rather have the puck carrier do—shoot or deke. Another way of looking at this is to consider what a goalie does better, stopping a direct shot or a deke. When the goalie knows that, he can try to play the breakaway in such a manner that he increases the chances that the puck carrier does what the goalie wants him to do.

Goalies who have success against breakaways are often able to anticipate them. They are not surprised by the breakaway, and they don't get caught moving out when the attacker is approaching. If certain teammates are prone to surrendering the puck in specific situations, the goalie must be alert to that possibility. Here are two typical situations that can lead to breakaways:

1. The defenseman coming out of the zone has a tendency to attempt a cross-zone pass when forecheckers are in position to intercept those passes.
2. The defenseman on the offensive blue line tends to take slap shots with his head down, often shooting into the legs of an opponent who is moving out to cover the point.

In these two instances, the goalie can almost predict the breakaway before it happens. To be ready, he must skate out to the top of the crease, maybe beyond, and prepare to play the lone break.

Coming Out and Gap Control

Once the goalie identifies the breakaway, he has to come out of the net and establish proper position. How far to come out depends on a number of factors, most notably how well the goalie skates and what the goalie wants the puck carrier to do. A better skater can come out more aggressively, safe in the knowledge that his skating ability will get him back quickly. If the goalie would rather face a deke, he should come out aggressively and all but eliminate the chances of a shot even being attempted, let alone finding open net. If he prefers to react to a shot, he wouldn't come out as far, thus increasing the likelihood that the puck carrier will shoot.

Next comes gap control. The goalie must maintain a constant distance between himself and the puck, which involves getting a sense of the puck carrier's speed. If he speeds up, the goalie speeds up; if he slows down, the goalie slows down. This maintains that constant distance, or gap. The purpose is to avoid either backing too far into the net or getting caught out so far that the puck carrier can easily skate around the goalie.

Next is the execution of the move. Against a deke, the goalie wants to force the puck carrier to make his A move. That is, a goalie doesn't want to get beaten along the ice on a deke, either between skate and post or through the legs (the 5 hole). The goalie should cover the entire ice by extending all the way to the post. If this is executed properly, the shooter can beat the goalie only by pulling the puck and lifting it at a fairly steep angle.

In a perfect situation, the goalie wants to remain centered on the puck even when leaving his feet in response to the deke. That means pushing off the far skate, bringing the stick to the puck, and maintaining control of the upper body, the chest still centered on the puck. This also means the goalie doesn't simply drop straight down and extend his skate toward the puck. He moves his entire body in a coordinated fashion, almost launching himself toward the post on the side the play moves to.

Against a shot, the goalie should be in good shape to make the save if he is correctly aligned on his angles, maintains good gap control, and doesn't drift back too deep in the crease. At some point, he must get set for the shot. The goalie must also note which way the puck carrier shoots, left or right. Should the puck be pulled to one side, the goalie must make the lateral adjustment to stay centered on the puck. Some young goalies back straight in toward the net, lining up more on the shooter's body than on the puck, which gives the shooter space to score on the stick side.

Other Factors

If the puck carrier approaches the goalie with his head down, the goalie has another option: the poke check. Goalies may be successful with this aggressive tactic if the puck carrier is ill equipped to see it coming. Conversely, if the puck carrier is a skilled player with his head up, the goalie should be reluctant to initiate such a move, since his opponent can see it and successfully react. The element of surprise is key, and a puck carrier with his head down allows for that. For example, the poke check is a good option when the puck carrier looks down at a puck that has rolled on edge. Goalies benefit by being aggressive in these situations.

There is also a difference between plays coming straight down the ice and breakaways from the side. The path of the puck carrier makes a difference. A player coming right at the goalie can go to either side, although most dekes are made to the backhand side. A player coming in from the side usually has two choices: shoot or cut across the front of the goal. Few players deliberately go short side or behind the net. In these situations, the goalie can almost force the attacker to cut across the front by taking the shot away. Then it's a matter of moving laterally with the attacker, which is difficult, or attacking either the puck or the space in front.

A goalie attacks the puck by attempting a poke check. He attacks space by attempting to claim an area, with the stick or a combination of stick and arm, to prevent the attacker from moving through that space. Given how difficult it is for a goalie at a dead stop to move laterally and match the speed of a player who already has momentum, the notion of attacking or claiming space is an attractive one. What ultimately determines the goalie's best option is the actual path of the attacker. If he is far from the goalie, say 10 to 20 feet, the goalie will have to move laterally on his feet. But if the attacker brings the puck within a stick's length of the goalie, then the goalie has the more aggressive option of attacking the puck or the space in front of the puck carrier's path.

Finally, there are breakaways that aren't clean. That is, a teammate is a factor at some point. If, for example, the puck carrier is coming in alone from the left wing and no defensive help is in sight, the goalie will have to be more cautious and patient. If the puck carrier is coming in from one side and a defensive teammate is hustling back into the play from the middle, this changes the time element of the play. Under pressure, the puck carrier will have less time and space to work with, and the goalie can factor that in, perhaps coming out more aggressively to one side knowing that if the attacker moves to the other side he'll be playing into the approaching teammate.

Coaches should allow goalies to work on all variations of breakaways and not just penalty shot or shootout types at the end of practice. Some breakaways begin just a few feet from a goalie, which doesn't give him time to get out and create that backward momentum. These should be practiced as well (see the breakaway drill).

Mini-Breakaway Drill

Place three shooters, each with a puck, about 15 to 25 feet from the goalie: one directly in front, one off to the left by the face-off dot, and one at the right dot. The coach stands behind the net and points to one of the puck carriers. Upon that silent signal, that player attacks the goal. The goalie won't know which attacker he must play until that player starts skating. Up to that point, the goalie must keep all three in sight with peripheral vision.

As an option, have a fourth player out behind this line of shooters. His job is to fill the slot vacated by the shooter. This way, you will always have three potential shooters at the start of each sequence.

Another option is to move the shooters who are on the two face-off dots deeper toward the goal line.

MENTAL SKILLS

The biggest challenge for many goalies is not how they move or react or play angles. For many it is dealing with the mental and emotional demands of the position. Consider the following:

- Forwards and defensemen take shifts of roughly 1 minute. Between shifts, they rest mind and body on the bench. Goalies stay on the ice for the entire game.

- Forwards and defensemen can make mistakes that are negated by the goaltender. The goaltender's mistakes are usually more obvious and often lead directly to goals.

- A forward may play poorly for most of the game but score a goal in the last minute and be a hero. The goaltender can have an outstanding game, but a soft goal at the end can make her a goat.

The speed of the game requires the goaltender to play without the burden of deliberation. A goalie wracked with self-doubt or a case of nerves is usually ineffective. Much like a referee, the goalie must perform without a tangible awareness of all that can go wrong. Both must have an unusually high degree of self-confidence to do the job well.

Confidence problems can be the result of a variety of situations. It could stem from fear of the unknown, such as a goalie moving up to a new level. It could be from fear of the known, such as recent poor performances. Or it could be from unrealistic expectations, established by themselves or by parents or coaches.

Coaches can't necessarily solve the problem, but they can make a situation worse. If a goalie is going through a tough stretch and dealing with confidence issues, a coach running a steady diet of one-on-none, two-on-none, and three-on-none drills at practice can certainly add to the problem.

A goalie's ability to control what she thinks about during competition helps her handle the mental demands of the game. Sport psychologists advise goalies to stay in the present. That is, don't think in the past (the last game, the last shot, the last time the team played this opponent), and don't let the mind race ahead to the future (the final score, what the coach will say in the locker room, what parents will say in the car, who will start the next game). Stay in the present. Concentrate on what is happening now. Another way to express this to a goalie is to tell her to focus on her efforts (now), not her results (later).

Some goalies accept the advice but don't know how to block the worries that come with poor play. Two typically worrisome situations for goalies are allowing a bad goal or seeing a lead turn into a deficit. Some goalies try to distract themselves by saying a positive phrase over and over. A goalie who tends to go down too early or often might say, "On your feet. On your feet." A goalie who tends to drift back too deep in the net might use, "One step out. One step out." In a sense, the goalie is displacing the potential bad thought with the mantra-like recitation of a positive sentiment.

CONCLUSION

For all the changes in goaltending, notably the improved equipment, the availability of private coaching, and a variety of new techniques when the puck is down low in the zone, the basics of playing the position really haven't changed in decades. It is still, first and foremost, about three things: being in the right place, controlling the puck, and having a sense of timing. The specific techniques a goalie chooses in order to accomplish those three objectives are individual choices. But these three primary areas must be mastered in order to play the position effectively.

To do this, a goaltender must understand where to be in a given situation (positioning), have the ability to get there under control (good movement skills, on and off the skates), have refined save techniques (puck control), and, finally, have a sense of knowing how to play the position (proper training).

The last skill is the most challenging. Many goalie coaches focus on teaching physical techniques, which is certainly necessary to play goalie well. But at higher levels of play, simply mastering a series of techniques is not the same as knowing how to play goalie. A goalie must understand the game of hockey—what opponents, with or without the puck, will do in certain situations; what teammates will do—and then process all this information to the point of seeing where everything will come together and when. Only then will a goalie begin to approach her highest level of competence.

11

Defensive Zone Play

Mark Dennehy

When asked why he robbed banks, famous 20th-century outlaw Willie Sutton reportedly responded, "Because that's where the money is." Although Sutton denied ever uttering those words, the quote has become part of American lore, even to the point of coining the phrase *Sutton's law* to identify a process that considers the obvious first.

In any discussion about prioritizing a hockey team's defensive zone play, a good starting point is to identify where goals are most commonly scored. Not surprisingly, the majority of goals are scored from the slot, the area between the face-off dots and below the hash marks. This area is so critical in the goal-scoring department that coaches and players often refer to it as "the house."

By contrast, it might come as a surprise that many scoring opportunities also originate from behind the goal line, with the goals perhaps scored directly from another spot, but the play being initiated from down low.

Therefore, defensive zone coverage begins with an obvious concept: protect the house, or the slot area. The defense's primary goal is to steer the puck into areas from which goals aren't scored. The defense seeks to contain the puck, put pressure on the puck carrier, and separate the player from the puck.

FIRST DEFENSIVE ZONE STRATEGY: SHRINK THE RINK

Defensive zone play is predicated on a couple of things. First, try to make it difficult for the opposing team to carry the puck into the zone. We want to force them to dump the puck into areas where we can pressure them. These areas are preferably in the corners where your players can outnumber the opponent and, in effect, shrink the rink by not giving them much

space. But it all begins and ends with the house, that area in front of the net where most goals are scored.

Once the puck is in one of the pressure zones, apply that pressure with the closest available defender, known as the contact player. Preferably this is the defenseman, but it could also be the center. She provides contact, and if she does a good job, the second person in, usually the center, gives support to either side.

The weak-side defender seals off any chance that the puck can come out of that corner and be carried toward the net. In the past, many coaches taught that the weak-side defenseman should begin at the far post and move toward the puck and the action in that corner. In today's game, you want that defenseman at that near post immediately.

The strong-side wing moves down to about the hash marks, and the weak-side wing moves down to about the same depth on the other side of the circle. Having all this support in a small area is what we call shrinking the rink, outnumbering the opponents and giving them very few opportunities to make plays. Hopefully, your team will also get the puck back.

Break this area into zones and give specific responsibilities to the wings. The wing on the boards covers from the boards to the dot, and the other wing covers the dot to the other side of the circle. Any opponent in these quadrants is that wing's responsibility. The wings also prevent the puck from getting back to opponents at the points (near the blue line).

These actions keep the puck from getting to the house, that dangerous area in front of the net. Players contain the puck by shrinking the rink, applying pressure through good stick-on-puck work, or otherwise neutralizing the opponents by pinning them against the boards. The intent is to separate the opponent from the puck in order to regain possession and start the attack. That is the goal of good defense.

Depending on how and where your team regains possession of the puck, players can send it around to the weak side and activate a breakout that way, or they can come directly up the strong side if that option is available.

INSTIGATING BREAKOUTS

Once you have possession of the puck, it's time to start building a breakout. First things first:

- The strong-side defenseman sprints back for the puck.
- Players must keep their heads on a swivel.
- The weak-side defenseman, the second guy back into the zone, needs to be aware of other threats, providing eyes and ears for the defenseman on the puck and shouting instructions.

Next, to effectively break out of the defensive zone, which is the key to avoid having to defend, the defensemen must be willing to take a hit to make a play. When your players are being forechecked, they want to break out on the weak side. Every once in a while, if someone can turn it up the ice directly and go, that's great. But when being pressured, players should get the puck to the weak side as quickly as possible.

There are two ways to do this. One is a simple corner-to-corner pass behind the net to the weak-side defenseman as the strong-side defenseman is being pressured (figure 11.1). This is called a bump. The puck-carrying defenseman will look for his partner to peel off into the corner for that pass once that weak-side defender makes certain his partner has the puck.

In figure 11.1, the attacking right wing (RW) is forechecking hard on the left defenseman (LD), who has the puck. In response to the pending

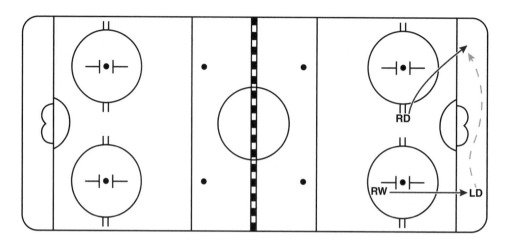

FIGURE 11.1 Corner-to-corner pass behind the net to the weak-side defenseman when the strong-side defenseman is under pressure.

pressure, the right defenseman (RD) moves behind the goal line to receive a bump pass from the LD. The pass is banked off the end boards.

One change made in recent years is to position the wings as close to the blue line as possible so they won't have too far to go to get the puck out of the zone when puck battles erupt there. With the wings high and the weak-side defenseman dropping down to be available for the bump pass, the center must come down low to provide support. You always want the center to be a source of support, but it is particularly important on the breakout.

The defenseman with the puck has to make a crucial read here. If he is under pressure from only a single forechecker, he will make that bump pass to his partner. But if he becomes aware of an aggressive forecheck from two opposing forwards, so that not only is he under pressure but his partner is as well, then he will do a hard wrap of the puck past his partner all the way to the weak-side wing (figure 11.2). After receiving the puck, the weak-side wing should have options, most notably the center curling up or the other wing cutting into the neutral zone for a pass. He can also chip it into the neutral zone, forcing opposing forwards to clear the offensive zone.

In figure 11.2, not only is the attacking right wing (RW) forechecking hard on the left defenseman (LD) who has the puck, but the attacking left wing (LW) is anticipating the pass to the weak-side defenseman (RD). In response to the pending pressure of two forecheckers down low, the LD sends the puck hard behind the net, deliberately past his partner and the second forechecker, with the intent that his RW will retrieve it and be able to break out on the far side.

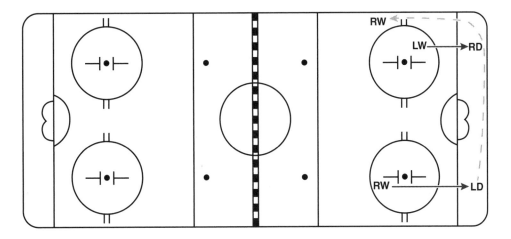

FIGURE 11.2 Defenseman executes a hard wrap of the puck to the weak-side wing.

The initial strong-side defenseman who has moved the puck—either by the bump or the wrap—should get himself up the ice as quickly as possible. You want four players on the rush whenever you can. Sometimes on the wrap it will be the weak-side defenseman who was not handling the puck who turns up ice first, rather than the first defenseman who had the puck. What is important is that you have at least four players transitioning to offense as quickly as possible.

In summary, the objectives of the breakout are as follows:

- The defensemen retreating to get the puck should be prepared to take a hit as they move the puck.

- The lead, or strong-side, defenseman must read which option is appropriate when moving the puck to the weak side: a bump pass to his partner when the partner is not under pressure or a full wrap around the boards to the weak-side wing, who is high in the zone when both defenseman are being pressured.

- As quickly as possible, at least one of the defensemen should jump up to join the offensive rush.

CONCLUSION

Defending the house is key to the success of a hockey team. Preventing the opposition from scoring goals requires a team effort. The defense needs to contain the puck, put pressure on the puck carrier, and, ultimately, gain possession of the puck. The defense wants to shrink the rink, forcing the offense to send the puck to spots where it's easy for the defense to pressure the puck and difficult for the offense to take a shot. When the defense can shrink the rink, it can get five defenders in the house, ready to make contact, pressure the puck carrier, and regain control. Once the defensemen have control of the puck, they can start a breakout to get the puck down the ice and perhaps set up a goal.

12

Neutral Zone Play

Ben Smith

If you were to survey youth coaches around the United States, you'd likely find that less attention, or at least later attention, is paid to teaching neutral zone play compared with offensive zone or defensive zone action.

Why is this the case? Every game begins with a center ice face-off, and much of the game's transitions, from offense to defense or defense to offense, take place in the neutral zone. At some point, coaches are well served by investing time in understanding what takes place in the neutral zone and devoting a sizable portion of their coaching curriculum to this area. Neutral zone play should be an extension of defensive zone breakouts. Starting practices with five-man breakouts with neutral zone regroups should be a daily exercise.

One reason the neutral zone may be overlooked is because there doesn't seem to be an immediate price to pay for mistakes made so far from either goal. But that mindset is flawed. Think of the old adage, "For want of a nail, the shoe was lost. For want of a shoe, the horse was lost. For want of a horse, a rider was lost. For want of a rider, a battle was lost. For want of a battle, the war was lost. And for want of a war, a nation was lost."

A small error in the neutral zone can lead to a turnover and a goal against, which may be the deciding goal in a game. If that game takes on greater meaning as the year goes along, well, you can lose a nation, or at least a season. This unraveling can begin with something as simple as how you line up on a neutral zone face-off and what happens when you lose a draw in the neutral zone.

NEUTRAL ZONE PLAY IN TODAY'S GAME

Coaches are conservative by nature. The basic premise they bring to a game—any game—is that they don't want to lose. Increasingly, similar to developments in soccer, coaches concentrate on defense first. It's certainly

easier to teach players, individually and as a team, to defend, to take away from the opponent, than it is to create offense.

So we see teams using passive forechecking systems, all the way to the now-famous neutral zone trap. In the trap scheme, defenders lie in wait in the middle of the ice, hoping to steer the offensive team into an area where they will be outnumbered, causing the offensive team to relinquish the puck by turning it over or dumping it into the opponent's defensive zone.

This is a recent development in hockey that makes the longstanding concept of head-manning the puck obsolete. Head-manning has been a common cry since the 1970s, when it was deemed selfish and unproductive for a player to lug the puck through the neutral zone instead of advancing it ahead to a waiting teammate. Today, that waiting teammate is usually stacked up against a wall of defenders who can strip him of the puck upon arrival. So coaches need to come up with creative ways to beat these neutral zone defenses.

Changes have also taken place in the way teams break out of their ends of the ice. With so many battles fought along the boards, the traditional clean breakout—with wingers moving wide and a center in the middle—is less likely to happen. The battles along the wall in the defensive end usually require weak-side wingers to come across and lend support, leaving a good section of the ice vacated. As the team breaking out gains the neutral zone, it needs to find a way to fill that open space, likely with the weak-side defenseman jumping up to be part of the offense.

RESPECTING THOSE LINES

Much of the significant action in the neutral zone takes place near the three lines that define it. I've told my teams, "Hey, guys, those lines aren't put there to make the rink colorful. Respect what happens there."

Turnovers happen at those lines for a reason. Offensive defensemen will aggressively attempt to keep a puck in the zone at the blue line. Teams breaking out of their end will often use the boards or glass just before approaching the near blue line to relieve the pressure from a forecheck or an aggressive defenseman. The puck carrier heading from his end knows that getting to the red line gives him the option of dumping the puck without getting called for icing, while the defenders tend to clog that area to prevent him from doing so. And when approaching the offensive blue line, speed and skill need to be in sync to prevent going offside, while defenders step up and make that particularly challenging.

Each of these areas presents the need for quick decision making by the puck carrier. Is it more important to retain possession of the puck or to regain or recapture a zone? We've all seen poor choices leading to problems in each of these areas, particularly at the blue lines. When a puck carrier coming out of his own end is the last person between his goalie and an enemy defender, stickhandling just inside the blue line is an unnecessary risk. Get stripped of the puck, and the opponent will have a clean breakaway. Whether you have a clean pass or not, getting the puck past the blue line and recapturing the zone may be your best option.

When a puck carrier approaches the offensive zone, he has options. Perhaps there is an open teammate ahead. Perhaps there is space to carry the puck into the offensive zone. But increasingly, defenders are stepping up, limiting the time for the puck carrier to approach this important space. So dumping the puck into the offensive zone is a good option to prevent a turnover that starts the opponent's next offensive attack.

As is the case in much of what we are laying out here, the situation at the moment (such as the score or time remaining) will likely influence which option the puck carrier chooses. It is easier to justify giving up possession of the puck and safely recapturing a zone when you are ahead on the scoreboard. The temptation to hold on to the puck may be greater as time winds down in the game and you find yourself needing a tying goal.

DEFENDING IN THE NEUTRAL ZONE

Most coaches think from their own net out, so let's look at neutral zone play when the other team has the puck. Often the neutral zone structure emanates from what kind of forecheck you employ. If you use a 1-2-2 forecheck in the offensive zone, you probably won't benefit from having a 1-3-1 in the neutral zone. You'll want to keep things consistent.

Among the primary factors that determine which type of forecheck you prefer are the skill levels of your players and the score of the game. For example, if you don't have a deeply talented team, you may opt for a more passive forecheck, using a 1-2-2 or even a 1-4, in a sense steering the opponent's puck carrier to one side and trapping him in that area. This is also a sound strategy when holding a lead. If, on the other hand, you find yourself trailing late in a game and needing a tying goal, you may want to employ a more aggressive 2-3 forecheck in the hope of forcing a turnover closer to the opponent's goal.

The same options are available after losing a neutral zone face-off when the puck goes back to an opposing defenseman. You either send one player at the puck or attack the two defensemen at once, depending on your overall philosophy of the game or what your immediate needs are. A single player who is forechecking should take a route to the defenseman that will take away the defenseman-to-defenseman pass. Two players who are forechecking can delay the second forward so that it is a safer forecheck. Some coaches call this a one and a half.

The goal here is to regain possession of the puck. This can be done by individual effort, largely through skilled use of stick and body to separate the puck from one player or to force a poor pass. It can also come from taking away space so effectively that teams are forced to dump the puck into your end of the ice, where your defensemen can go back and retrieve it.

By creating a turnover in the zone, you immediately move from defense to offense. Being skilled in this transition is what separates average teams from those squads that are special. Teams with a good offensive transition can generate a quick-strike attack, one featuring speed entering the zone and plenty of options for the puck carrier.

CREATING OFFENSE THROUGH AND IN THE NEUTRAL ZONE

Offensive attacks can move through the neutral zone after a successful breakout or can be started in the neutral zone after a turnover and transition. In each instance, the puck carrier needs support (a player or players to pass to), and the attack itself needs speed, width, and, increasingly, depth to be successful.

Teams can't always expect to break out of their zones with the three forwards skating in distinct lanes, trailed by the defense. This may be how we draw it up at practice, but games are rarely that structured. Battles in the defensive zone often lead to weak-side support coming across the zone to help, leaving the other side of the ice empty. Aggressive neutral zone defenses force the attack to one side of the ice or the other. In the face of these realities, offensive attacks often need defensemen to jump up into those open areas and help provide the desired width of the attack.

The depth factor comes when the offensive attack gets the puck into the zone, either by a player carrying the puck in or by quick puck movement (passing). As defenders focus on this first wave of the attack, the puck carrier should be able to pick up one or more trailing teammates entering the zone to complete the attack.

These opportunities aren't always going to be there, as indicated by the increasingly effective use of passive or trapping defenses in the neutral zone. As a result, teams need to develop specific dump-in strategies. Some coaches like to rim the puck around the boards. Others prefer a cross-corner dump-in. Still others like to put the puck directly on goal. Your choice will depend on what you know about your own strengths and perhaps your opponent's weaknesses. If, for example, the opposing goalie doesn't handle the puck well, make him handle it.

REGROUPING

So far, we have looked at plays that go in a straight line from defensive zone to offensive zone. But watch any hockey game today and you'll quickly realize this doesn't always happen. Most teams who retain or regain possession of the puck in the neutral zone don't feel obligated to force the play if they don't like what they see ahead. Instead, they'll reverse themselves and regroup with the hope that they can create a better attack.

The concept of regrouping was learned from the Soviets in the 1970s. Although this strategy was on display when North American clubs increased their competition against the great Soviet Union teams of that era, a good deal of credit should go to Lou Vairo, one of the most underappreciated coaches the United States has ever produced.

Vairo came to public attention when he was chosen to coach the 1984 U.S. Olympic team. But long before Vairo received that plum assignment, he had caught the attention of certain people high in the USA Hockey coaching pyramid who understood that Vairo was onto something.

Years earlier, Vairo had forged a friendship with legendary Soviet coach Anatoli Tarasov. Visiting Russia and enjoying unusual access to Tarasov and his methods, Vairo learned the Soviet tactics and brought them home, where he incorporated much of what he learned with his teams, most notably the Austin Mavericks junior team.

Coaches began to hear about this guy from New York who was teaching new and exciting concepts in Austin. One of those coaches was Herb Brooks. Although little has been acknowledged, much of the 1980 U.S. Olympic team's success can be attributed to what Vairo shared with Brooks and others. Now, decades later, you can find everyone from your local mite team to squads in the over-50 women's league using a center ice regroup to start an offensive attack.

In a typical regroup, the forward progress is reversed with a pass back to one of the defensemen behind the play. The defenseman with the puck usually moves laterally in one direction while her partner swings behind in the other, ready to receive a defenseman-to-defenseman pass. This is called *hinging*. The center comes back, facing the defense, creating a triangle with them and providing the defensemen with another passing outlet. In this sense, the triangle created by the center and two defensemen is very similar to the triangles that a center and the two wingers look to create in the offensive zone, which is one of the earliest basic formations that players and coaches learn. However, the defensive zone regroup shows that the concept of triangulation isn't limited to the offensive zone.

During a defensive zone regroup, while the defensemen play catch, either with each other or with the center, the wingers need to get open. One can jump ahead to the neutral zone and stretch the defense. The other might cut across the ice, attracting defenders and opening up space for others to fill. Too often at youth levels, wingers get ahead of the puck and come to a halt at the blue line. These forwards are not particularly helpful when they're standing still and away from the puck carrier.

"Where do I go, coach?" I have heard this from my middle school team plenty of times. "I don't care," I'll say. "Keep moving and get open."

One way to look at an effective regroup is to liken it to your breakout. Look at figures 12.1 and 12.2. One shows a breakout and one shows a neutral zone regroup. They are basically the same. In the latter, just picture the net being on the near blue line, and imagine the five teammates acting similarly in each zone.

NEUTRAL ZONE AND THE RULE BOOK

Many hockey fans praise the day the so-called tag-up rule came into being. At elite levels, when defensemen dump the puck back into the offensive zone with one or more of their teammates still there, there is no need to worry. As long as those teammates don't touch the puck, they can get back to the blue line, tag up, and then go right back in on the forecheck. Play continues. No whistles. Everyone is happy.

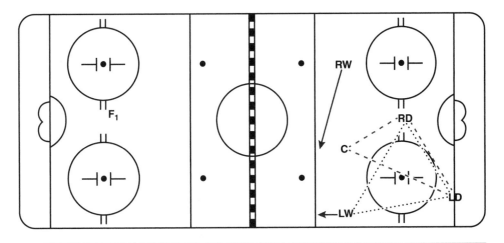

FIGURE 12.1 Breakout.

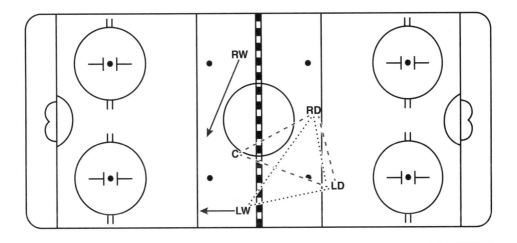

FIGURE 12.2 Neutral zone regroup.

So why were battle lines drawn a few years back when some members of the youth hockey community wanted the same rules to apply to them? No one wants whistles. Why can't we just dump it in and clear the zone, too?

The answer came from those of us who saw what the tag-up rule would do to skill development in youth hockey. No one would ever have any incentive to learn how to maintain possession of the puck, either through stickhandling or, even better, through a series of short passes made forehand to forehand while teammates took the time to clear the zone and avoid being offside. The tag-up rule at youth levels simply dumbs down the game and removes an incentive for developing good puckhandling and passing skills.

Which leads me back to regrouping. Today's game doesn't come with an earlier era's need to always move forward. What the Soviets first showed us 40 years ago has become a common philosophy today: If you don't like what you see going forward, drop the puck back and start over. And you can see the results.

What team practice, at virtually any level, doesn't include a regrouping drill today? Moving the puck back to the defense, defenseman-to-defenseman passing, center curls, wingers crossing, and the like. What skills are needed to run this effectively? The ability to make quick, accurate forehand-to-forehand passes in small areas buys time and allows for everyone to regroup. Coaches should always consider as part of their weekly drill collection some sort of controlled, small-area passing drills, with an emphasis on one-touch passing, forehand to forehand. Equally important is learning how to receive a pass, including those that may go awry.

Major concepts in neutral zone and transition play include the following:

- Make sure defensive pairings are comfortable with each other. If one defenseman is on his off hand (i.e., left-hand shot on the right side), it's important that he always present his forehand to his partner so the two can pass to one another without fumbling the puck.

- Verbal communication is vital. The defenseman without the puck should always be instructing his partner and not simply watching.

- The two wingers should also present their forehands to all teammates.

- Wingers should switch with their center when they see the center coming to their side of the ice, thus taking the center's position.

BONUS POINTS

I suggested earlier that many coaches might not emphasize neutral zone play because the area is far from anything that can immediately become a problem. But that's not necessarily true, especially when you realize that one small mistake can lead to defensive breakdowns.

In the 2014 Stanley Cup Eastern Conference final series, the New York Rangers took a lead late in the second period of game four when Montreal got caught in a sloppy line change. The Rangers' Dan Girardi, standing inside his own blue line, saw that Montreal was changing on the fly and that teammate Derick Brassard was breaking through the neutral zone into vacated space at the far blue line. Girardi's 80-foot pass went tape to tape, sending Brassard in alone on Dustin Tokarski, who was promptly beaten by a slap shot with less than a minute to play in the second.

Although I'm frequently amazed by the lack of discipline shown when players decide to change up with the puck in their defensive zone, this example shows how the relative calm of the neutral zone can lull a team into a game-changing mistake. The Montreal defenseman, who chose this moment to change, failed to read the immediate danger he was creating in a 1-1 tie. Although the Canadiens would tie the game at 2-2 in the third period, they eventually lost this game in overtime.

Stretching the Defense

The term *stretching the defense* is used in a number of sports, most notably in football when a speedy wide receiver forces one or more defensive backs to follow him down the field. It can also be seen in hockey, although not with the same frequency.

To create more open space, teams breaking out of their zones will sometimes send a forward down the ice and deliberately offside into the offensive zone. A defender is sure to follow this attacker, at least to his own blue line. The offensive player will, out of necessity, come back into the neutral zone, usually facing his oncoming teammates and in a position to receive a pass, which he would likely one-touch to a streaking forward or back to where it originated.

Note the stretch player is seldom the target. His purpose is to open up space in soft, safe areas in which shorter passes can be completed, leaving the defender who went with that stretch player caught between a rock and a hard place. If the defender moves up (or gaps up), he is skating straight at the oncoming attack and can be easily juked. If he stays back at the blue line, he will have to play the rush somewhat flat-footed.

This is not unlike a dynamic we see in football in which a star wide receiver goes deep, taking a defender (or two) with him. Often, he is not the intended receiver. He just takes people with him to create space, so shorter passes can be completed to someone else.

Taking Neutral Zone Face-Offs

Finally, let me give a little attention to neutral zone face-offs. Specifically, let's look at two neutral zone face-offs designed to create a quick strike.

In figure 12.3, the left winger (LW) heads to the near boards when his center wins the draw back to the left defender (LD). As the opposing team's right winger (X1) approaches the left winger, he bursts across the zone and attempts to receive a pass as he splits the opposing defense. This is a face-off play the Boston Bruins have employed in recent years with left winger Brad Marchand.

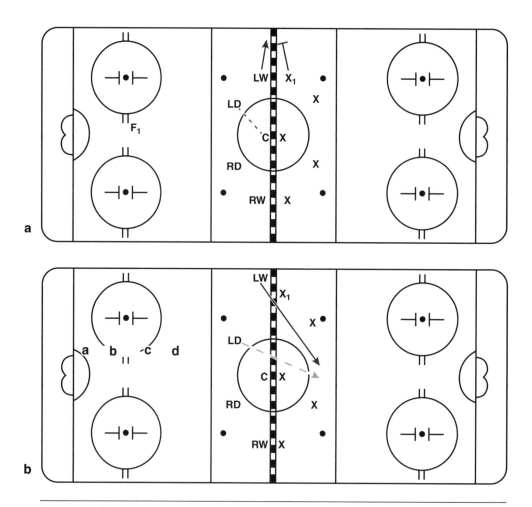

FIGURE 12.3 Neutral zone face-off play used by the Boston Bruins: *(a)* LW moves to boards; *(b)* as opponent's RW approaches, LW splits the defense to receive a pass.

Figure 12.4 makes me recall a very specific situation. I was coaching with former NHL and USA Hockey head coach Ron Wilson when we found ourselves down a goal late in the game and on a power play. In this instance, we lined up four people across with only one defenseman behind. The right winger here was split wide and did a little selling by yelling from that spot to get the opponent's attention. The defense shifted toward the RW.

As our left-shot center won the draw back to our defenseman, our right winger cut left across the zone, bringing one, maybe two defenders with him and, in the process, opening up the entire right side. Our left winger cut across as shown into that newly vacated lane and took a pass from our left defender. He went in and got a great shot on goal, if I remember correctly.

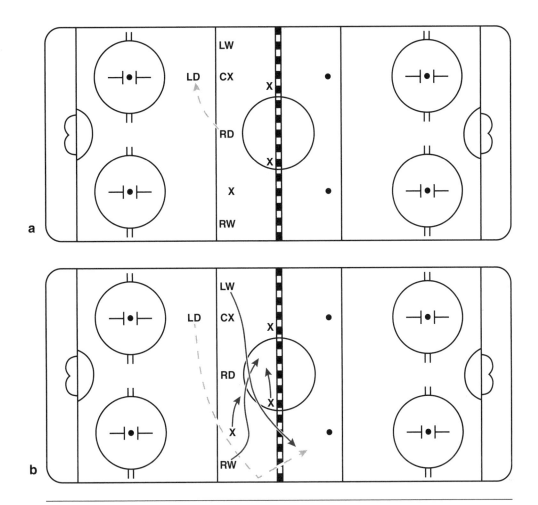

FIGURE 12.4 Neutral zone face-off with four across and LD behind: *(a)* RW split wide; *(b)* when defense shifted to RW, he cut left across the zone and opened up the right side for the LW to enter and receive a pass.

CONCLUSION

The most important role in the transition game, however, belongs to the center. Centers have a big responsibility. They must be the connection for transition from defense to offense. Centers must support the defensemen and also the two wingers as the play moves up the ice. From the center ice face-off, the center must be the conduit that allows all five skaters to stay connected. The center should always be facing the puck so possession can be ensured. The team that has the puck the majority of the time will have the best chance of success.

13

Offensive Zone Attack

E.J. McGuire

In 1951, hockey pioneer Lloyd Percival wrote in *The Hockey Handbook*, "The development of the tactical and strategical elements of hockey is probably still on a fairly low level. So far it has not undergone the high level 'brain trusting' that contributed and continues to contribute so much to such games as baseball, football, and basketball. There are those who claim that hockey offers no parallel, that it is too fast moving, with unforeseen situations developing all the time. As much could be said about basketball! The subject of strategy and tactics in offensive play must be considered in relation to the individual player as well as in relation to the team." It's been more than half a century since *The Hockey Handbook* introduced concepts that were then considered radical but are now celebrated as being ahead of their time. Although Percival had to analyze single-frame photographs of hockey game action, the technology used now can instantaneously recall the most minute detail and display replays from multiple angles with crystal clear video detail. However, some observers lament that along with these advancements has come the simultaneous smothering of creative, exciting, offensive hockey.

Modern technology and sophisticated specialization in the coaching profession have led Stanley Cup winner and Hall of Fame coach Scotty Bowman to assert that these are the primary reasons defensive systems and strategies have outpaced offensive hockey. Simply, it's easier to design and implement defensive alignments than it is to teach the creative, flashy play that creates offensive scoring opportunities. The resulting imbalance of defense over offense had rule makers in the mid-2000s scrambling to impose legislation to restore some of the offensive elements that made the game the exciting spectacle it had become over the years.

All the rule changes, proposals, and pleas for a more offensively exciting game were designed to promote a return to some of the fundamentals of the sport. The goal is to enhance the simple act of taking the puck with speed into the high-percentage scoring areas and creatively launching an attack. These are not revolutionary concepts. This chapter summarizes the key fundamentals of offensive zone attack.

SPEED

Speed is the essence of hockey. It is never more important than in the composition of a good offensive attack. Although I implied that good defensive posture and positioning are the antithesis of offensive opportunities, the transition from good defensive positioning to offense is greatly aided by the spreading of defenders, which is one of the fundamentals of good defensive zone coverage. The resulting staggered charge of attacking players coming from that defensive zone coverage can be most advantageous to a successful rush up the ice. Spreading out the offensive attackers reduces the ability of the defenders to channel, funnel, or trap the offense into a confined area of the ice. Therefore, good offense can indeed be launched from good defense.

The basic hockey skill of outright skating speed is an offensive weapon that can force any defense to back off even more. However, it is not the speed of the players but more fundamentally the speed of the puck that can break down defenses. This was a critical concept adopted by the great Russian coach Anatoli Tarasov, regarded as the founding father of Soviet hockey. As he was developing his Red Army teams behind the secrecy provided by the Cold War's Iron Curtain, he noted in his book *Road to Olympus*, "We shall have to build up our so-called 'first attack' because the speed of developing an attack (or counterattack) is equal to the speed of the puck in motion. And by accurately passing to each other, our forwards manage to outplay their opponents, thereby giving themselves numerical superiority in the enemy zone" (1969, 155).

ENTRIES

Score off the rush, but don't be in a rush to score! Use the speed you've generated via quick transition through the neutral zone to move the puck directly into the prime scoring area. Generate the best shot possible on goal, with players going to the net for deflections and screens before the puck gets there, and following the shot in anticipation of a rebound if the initial shot attempt gets blocked en route to the net. It sounds simple.

Most defenses facing a speedy or odd-man-advantage attack will instinctively protect the center of the ice, so entry is most often successful when the attackers plan to cross the blue line with the puck on the wings, near one of the side boards. A key teaching point for a puck carrier is to emphasize moving the puck north–south through that offside area within five feet of either side of the offensive blue line. Gaining entry directly allows for other attackers to support the rush without any speed restrictions due to the fear of going offside.

The concept of triangulation can create space in the most opportune ice area. A wide drive by the puck carrier should be supported by a teammate on his side of the ice. If a direct path to the net is cut off, the support player becomes the primary target for a pass. The puck carrier should continue his drive to the net as one point of the offensive triangle (figure 13.1). His decision to shoot is determined by whether he can gain a satisfactory location on the scoring web. The second wave of support comes from the third point on the offensive triangle.

Often the preceding scenario doesn't present itself as readily as the coach's rink diagrams might suggest. Tarasov felt the pre-1970s game in North America was flawed, citing, "The main thing in the attack of professionals is surprise, timing, a desire to crush the opponent with a terrific rush" (1969, 155).

Creative offensive teams are schooled to allow even more support to come in behind the offensive triangle threesome. A tight turn toward the side boards (figure 13.2) usually creates time and space for the puck carrier to locate a fourth teammate, often a defenseman who has hustled to beat his backchecking opponents into a prime scoring area vacated by the passage through the offensive triangle. The delay play—a turn-up or tight-turn maneuver by the puck carrier—most often is a pass to a trailing

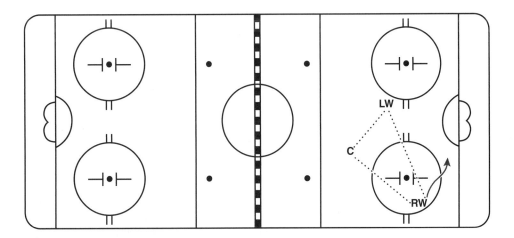

FIGURE 13.1 Offensive triangle with the puck carrier (RW) driving to the net, the center (C) coming into the zone on the same side for support, and the left winger (LW) driving to the net for additional support.

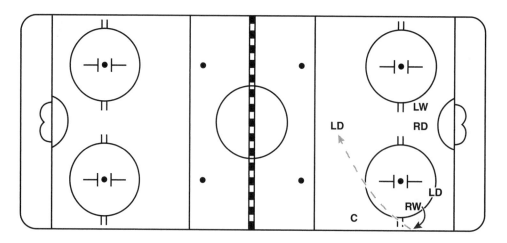

FIGURE 13.2   His path to the net cut off, the puck carrier (RW) makes a tight turn to the boards. Additional support for the offensive attack frequently comes from a defenseman (LD) who enters the zone behind the three forwards.

defenseman, often in the area just inside the blue line, as defenders focus on the more traditional scoring areas closer to the goal.

Other common methods of entry include either a chip by the defender or a dump in and recovery operation (figures 13.3 to 13.5). Hockey purists are reticent to give up possession when their team already has worked hard to attain it. Indeed, turning the puck back in the neutral zone and executing a regroup maneuver remains a viable alternative. These are more frequently seen in the European-style game, where the larger Olympic-size ice surfaces can contribute to more of a puck-control philosophy, but regrouping is slowly becoming more popular in North American-style play.

The chip-by or dump-and-chase plays are executed with the purpose of a quick and efficient recovery. Beginning with the 2005-2006 season, the NHL instituted a pair of changes that may have a positive effect on this playing style. The first is the limitation on where the goaltender is allowed to handle the puck outside of his crease. A cross-corner dump-and-chase (figure 13.4) and a soft dump to the corner (figure 13.5) now go to an area where, in the past, the goaltender could come out and retrieve the puck, with little chance of being forechecked effectively. Because of the adopted trapezoid area behind the goal line, which limits where the goalie is allowed to play the puck, these corner areas now become a place where races to the loose puck are contested, and battles for down-low possession result.

The second NHL change is not related to the playing rules but rather to the configuration of the end zones. The goal line has been returned to its pre–1998-1999 position of 11 feet (rather than 13 feet) from the end

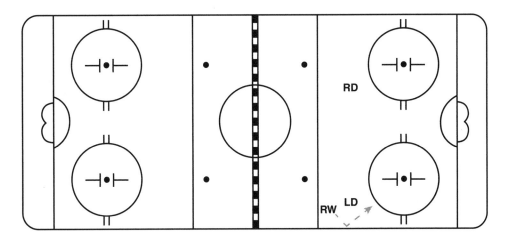

FIGURE 13.3 A simple chip off the boards is followed by a race to the puck between the RW and the LD. New rules prevent the defenseman from making contact in an attempt to slow down the attacker.

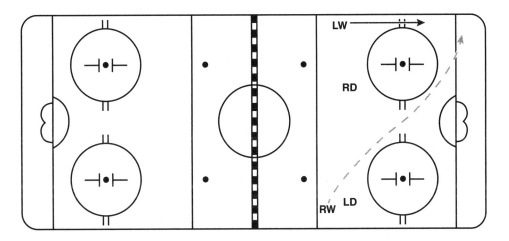

FIGURE 13.4 In this option, the puck carrier dumps the puck into the opposite corner, where his teammate (LW) is likely to be the first on the puck in a race with the opponent's RD.

boards. The blue lines have been pushed 2 feet closer to center, making shots from the blue line to the goal line now 64 feet. The youth hockey playing rules, governed independently in North America by USA Hockey and Hockey Canada, and U.S. college hockey, governed by the NCAA, have yet to adopt any of these changes.

It may take several years to determine the positive effect, if any, of this added space in the attacking zone on creating more offense. But it seems that the chip-by entry maneuver illustrated in figure 13.3 now benefits

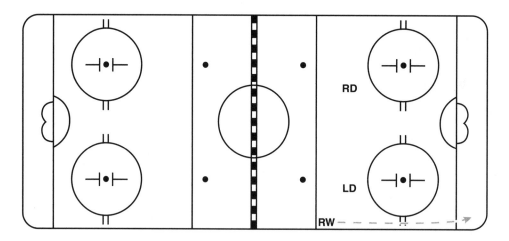

FIGURE 13.5 In this option, the puck carrier (RW) makes what is called a soft dump, intending for the puck to stay in that near corner as he chases it, as opposed to shooting hard around the net.

from the added space along the side boards. The key, in addition to the underlying speed of the rush and entry, is anticipation and puck support. A mental attitude for winning the battles for puck recovery in that contested area, combined with the refined ability to steal and control the puck in tight quarters, is obviously critical for offensive success.

SETTING UP

Anatoli Tarasov, the Russian master coach and strategist, offered his opinion in his start-from-scratch analysis of how he could quickly develop the Soviet hockey program into a global power, and indeed, for a time in international hockey, lead them to world dominance: "An attack should be built more rationally; of course, the enemy net should be attacked swiftly and skillfully. We frown upon reckless hockey. This is not a scientific approach to hockey, accurate and reasonable playing" (1969, 155). In the 2000s, however, the game has morphed into a far different game. Aside from man-advantage situations (and even then not often), the offensive team is rarely afforded the time or space to employ any preset designs. As a result, today's practices should be designed to drill and perfect the spontaneous, subconscious ability to quickly recognize and exploit any momentary weakness in the opposition's defensive zone coverage. This can be achieved most effectively by players with a take-it-to-the-net mentality. Coaches should have their players drilled to move quickly into a more advantageous position in the offensive scoring web and to strike during the split second a defensive breakdown is sensed.

DOWN-LOW OFFENSE: CYCLING

The ability of the attacking team to possess and protect the puck while waiting for a defensive breakdown and subsequent offensive opportunity has been referred to in recent hockey parlance as *cycling*. Perfecting this tactic requires generous amounts of both basic hockey skills and patience. An awareness of open, uncontested areas of the offensive zone, often referred to as quiet zones, helps in chipping or moving the puck to areas of teammate support. A visual example of such a play is depicted in figure 13.6.

Since time constraints and opposition pressure often dictate that the puck be delivered to the quiet zone support area before a teammate gets there, cycling success obviously depends on superior anticipation and communication. That communication can be either verbal or nonverbal. Correctly predicting a teammate's placement of the puck in the quiet zone is referred to as having superior (or well-practiced) reading skills. Another key teaching point in cycling is to have players reappear in the quiet zones, even if they didn't receive these spot passes the first time through. Smart players present themselves as passing options more than once in the same sequence.

You could argue that offensive zone cycling, in and of itself, is not an offensive tactic at all unless the end result (or at least the ultimate goal) is generating a scoring chance. Although some situations in a game may warrant delay tactics (such as killing a penalty or running down the clock while protecting a late third-period lead), the take-it-to-the-net mentality should prevail at the first hint of a defensive breakdown.

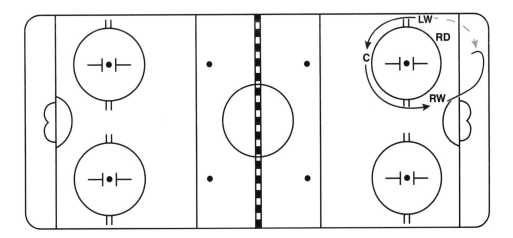

FIGURE 13.6   The LW turns from the boards and his defender (RD). In the middle of his turn, he leaves the puck behind his path for his RW, who is circling (or cycling) around the face-off circle. The RW will attempt the same maneuver, leaving the puck for the center (C).

OFFENSIVE FACE-OFFS

The one time in hockey when preset formations and designed plays can start from scratch is during face-offs. Possession of the puck is critical. NHL coaching veterans Mike Murphy and Mike Kitchen devoted a major portion of a coaching symposium to strategies and tactics for successful face-offs.

The offensive center has three options: Draw the puck back to a teammate in the slot or at the near point, tie up the opposing center in hopes that a teammate can come in and retrieve the loose puck, or attempt to drive the puck directly on net from the draw. In all these cases, teams must work hard at practice to get their timing down and (for the players away from the puck) to tie up defenders. And of course, in the end, it all turns on the center's ability to win the face-off.

In recent years, many referees have been instructed to watch out for face-off interference, where offensive players deny defenders a legitimate path to the puck off a face-off. This tactic can be subtle or obvious, and it challenges officials at all levels.

The effectiveness of these plays in producing a scoring chance depends in large part on recognizing what might work versus the opponent's defensive face-off alignment. Scouting reports may also suggest vulnerabilities in the tendencies of the opposition's centers. Predetermined signals can be effective, similar to an audible called by a football quarterback as he scans the defense at the line of scrimmage.

ADOPT AN OFFENSIVE MINDSET

As much as on-ice skill development drills are critical to fundamental offensive hockey, an underlying theme of this chapter has been adopting a mentality of getting to the scoring areas and eventually getting the puck to the net. Players can practice visualizing themselves in goal-scoring situations off the ice. Indeed, since scoring is the most enjoyable part of the game, a more accurate statement might be that players should probably always be thinking about it.

Players do this almost automatically. The better ones, it's been suggested, do it more frequently and more vividly. Coaches need to support this off-ice mental practice as a means of attaining goals.

Recent advancements in the field of sport psychology have addressed and investigated this area of mental imagery as a performance-enhancement technique. Literature suggests a number of the positive effects of mental imaging on skills, tactical strategies, performance execution, and error correction. Former NHL defenseman Eric Weinrich, a veteran of 18 seasons after graduating from the University of Maine, was considered an offensive defenseman throughout his career, often quarterbacking his team's power play from the point. He attests to the value of mental training but relies on it more as an off-ice preparation routine: "During the game, I don't visualize much when I am on the bench. All the work should have been done ahead of time. . . I trust in my ability and my experience to get the job done. If you do the practice and mental rehearsal regularly beforehand, your performance in the game will be fine" (Hale et al. 2005, 131).

Coaches can reinforce performance enhancement in many ways, such as seeking out a person with experience in this mental practice to work with the team. Building an offensive mindset could then be a shared theme of both the sport psychology consultant and the coaching staff. More directly, the head coach should consider changing the behind-the-bench mentality toward a more proactive atmosphere of seeing solutions rather than barking orders meant to correct on-ice mistakes or yelling from the bench to try to influence officiating decisions.

OFFENSIVE GAME TACTICS

Much of the resurrection of more creative offensive thinking in hockey was facilitated by the NHL lockout season of 2004-2005. Coaches such as Dave King, current St. Louis Blues head coach Ken Hitchcock, and others devoted their unexpected free time to studying the game from several in-depth angles not available to them during a regular working season. Former Phoenix Coyotes associate coach and current director of player personnel for the Chicago Blackhawks, Barry Smith, has studied the tactics and philosophy of hockey as it is taught in the Czech Republic, conferring with renowned national coach Dr. Ludek Bukac. Smith came away with several suggestions for how the North American game can reinject the excitement into a sport that has seemingly lost its underpinnings of offensive creativity.

The following ideas warrant consideration regarding the offensive aspect of the game:

◆ Confine practice drills to smaller areas of the ice. Conduct several simultaneous drills using perhaps one-third of the allotted rink space rather than full-ice drills.

◆ Place more emphasis on high-tempo speed drills.

◆ Shorten the duration of each drill. Have bursts of practice that contain finite, skill-specific drills such as a skating-only emphasis, passing-only emphasis, and puckhandling-only emphasis instead of the multiple-skill full-ice drills that currently consume so much valuable practice time.

◆ Practice inverse-ratio activities (2v1, 3v2, 4v3, and so on) to accelerate skill development under adverse conditions. Controlled scrimmages can be conducted under these conditions as well; the team with the manpower advantage is not allowed to employ any of the traditional setup formations similar to power play situations. For example, once the team with the additional player gains the offensive zone, that team is limited to only two passes before a shot must be taken.

◆ Abandon the traditional notion of set positions. Allow players to interchange positions. Allow even the fifth player to join the offense in this interchange.

◆ Employ an offensive coordinator. The role of the offensive coordinator is tantamount to overcoaching such fundamentals as keeping the feet moving, moving the puck quicker, making yourself a passing option, maintaining speed, and so on.

If hockey is to continue to flourish as both a spectacle for fans and, more important, a fun activity for players, we must emphasize the most exciting aspects of the game in offensive zone attacks.

CONCLUSION

Offensive opportunities are created by players away from the puck finding open space and using speed to put pressure on the defense. The ability to enter the zone wide and create an offensive triangle is a basic of offensive play that remains relevant today.

Coaches need to be aware of defensive tendencies, as well as changes in the rules of the game, to make sure their offensive philosophy and tactics are suited for the modern game. Regarding the latter, as attacking players can no longer be held up by defenders for fear of tighter interference calls, puck carriers have the option of "chipping" pucks into the zone and attacking the puck with greater speed than before.

Hockey games are won by winning a series of small battles. Accordingly, using small area games at practices will prepare teams for game-day battles that can lead to better puck control and improved offensive play.

REFERENCES

Hale, B.D., L. Seiser, E.J. McGuire, and E. Weinrich. 2005. Mental imagery. In *Applying sport psychology: Four perspectives*, ed. J. Taylor and G.S. Wilson, 117-135. Champaign, IL: Human Kinetics.

Percival, L. 1951. *The Hockey Handbook*. New York: Barnes.

Tarasov, A. 1969. *Road to Olympus*. Toronto: Griffin House.

14

Special Teams and Situations

George Gwozdecky and Michael Zucker

Since the NHL lockout in the 2004-2005 season, the league has cracked down on penalties such as holding, hooking, and interference, and it has slowly trickled down into the college, junior, and youth hockey leagues. This initiative has changed the way the game is played by creating a greater emphasis on skill and speed. In addition, it has created a larger focus on the power play and the penalty kill. This has forced coaches to spend considerable time developing and practicing special-team strategies because of their impact on today's game.

Your plan for special teams should focus on realistic, age-appropriate systems in order to maximize each player's potential while putting players in situations in which they can be successful. Simply because a specific power-play breakout works for the Detroit Red Wings is no indication it will work for your peewee youth team.

Coaches watch a lot of hockey and pick up many helpful tactics and systems from various levels. Understanding how to break down these systems into simple concepts is critical for helping players understand and properly execute the plan. Every time a new system is taught, whether it is special teams or even strength, identify the concepts and basic skills required to execute the system. Then develop drills or small games to emphasize those points.

A simple example supporting the analysis of a system can be illustrated in the power-play breakout. In most power-play breakouts, a defenseman will pick up the puck behind the net, skate a few strides with the puck, and then make a pass to a supporting forward who is on the wall or cutting across the ice toward the center. Looking at this basic system on a more granular level shows several skills required by the defenseman in order to accomplish a successful breakout pass.

For one, the defenseman must surround the puck by getting his feet around it while moving it quickly to his forehand, regardless of whether he collects it from along the boards or in open ice. A defenseman must also look back over his shoulder, or shoulder check, to determine if oncoming pressure is being applied by the forechecking team. Last, a defenseman must use the net as an obstacle to fend off the opposing forechecker. These are three skills important for a defenseman's success, and he hasn't even attempted to pass the puck yet.

CHOOSING PERSONNEL

At the higher levels of hockey, a significant amount of time is spent determining the correct personnel to use for a team's power-play units. Initially this is done by looking at each individual player and assessing strengths and weaknesses, which will eventually lead to your creating units of five players whose strengths will complement one another. Youth coaches may not have the luxury of assembling two equally talented units. However, strengths exist on each team, and with a little creativity, support players can fill in or supplement the top two or three players. This tactic is even used at the NCAA and NHL levels.

When the Detroit Red Wings ran their power-play breakout during the Nick Lidstrom era, they intentionally tried to get the puck into Lidstrom's hands because they knew he had the best chance of making a successful first pass up the ice. In addition, this first pass wasn't intended to end up in Johan Franzen's hands: The targets were either Pavel Datsyuk or Henrik Zetterberg. Franzen's role on that first power-play unit was not to carry the puck up the ice or make fancy plays in the neutral zone. His role began once his unit gained entry into the offensive zone, and that was to screen the goalie and score rebound goals, two jobs that fit his strengths perfectly.

This example shows the various types of players in the NHL, which translates down through the youth hockey levels as well. Certain players have vision and the ability to pass the puck or make plays. Others may have strength or size, while others have a natural ability to shoot the puck and score goals. The coach's challenge is to create a power-play unit (or units) while taking each of these factors into consideration.

Typically, the creation of a power-play unit starts with your best player. Ask yourself the following questions: Where do I see this player being most productive on the power play? Does he have the speed and skill to carry the puck up ice, or is he more of a playmaker? Will he show poise and have the ability to make quick decisions under pressure, or does he need more time and space to make the right play? Depending on the maturity level of the player, these issues can be discussed with the player directly.

A player who requires more time and space will likely have more success playing at the point by the blue line. A player with tenacity and the ability to battle for loose pucks will have the most success playing down low when the power play is set up in the zone. Good coaches can identify their players' tendencies and place them in the right position on the ice for the best chance of success.

DEVELOPING THE BREAKOUT

There are countless ways to diagram player positions on a power-play breakout. In most cases, however, the simplest ones tend to be the most effective, especially at the youth levels. The purpose of the power-play breakout is simple: to gain entry into the offensive zone with puck possession and puck support. Too often at the youth levels, coaches try to devise intricate power-play breakouts containing long, home-run type passes or low-percentage passes over 20 feet. These passes are difficult enough for many players at the higher levels and become even more difficult (if not impossible) for most youth players.

Instead of focusing on long, low-percentage passes, construct a power-play breakout that takes advantage of the uneven situation on the ice. This can be accomplished by isolating one of the opposing players and creating a two on one somewhere on the ice during the breakout, regardless of in which zone it occurs. Once zone entry is gained, the other line rush or offensive zone setup concepts will take over, so it is imperative to develop a simple, efficient power-play breakout in order to give your team the best chance to gain entry into the offensive zone.

Adjusting Your Power-Play Breakout to the Penalty-Kill Forecheck

Many coaches think of coaching hockey as similar to a chess match: You create a strategy, your opponent reacts to your strategy and defends against it, and you both continue to make adjustments in an attempt to stay one step ahead of the opposing coaching staff. Although this approach is more prevalent at higher levels, it is certainly relevant in youth hockey as well. Power-play breakouts should be developed with the opposing team's penalty kill forecheck in mind in order to have the most success.

With a man advantage on the power play, the goal is to try to create two-on-one situations, both on the breakout and while setting up in the offensive zone, in order to create a scoring chance. Regardless of the team's penalty-kill forecheck, the power-play breakout should attempt to freeze or trap the first forechecker. This is done by having your puck carriers hold onto the puck until they're pressured by a forechecker. Only then will they look to pass it while catching the opposing forechecker out of position or trapping him.

Over the years, very few *new* penalty-kill forecheck formations have been created. Let's review some of the more commonly seen penalty-kill forechecks and then some power-play breakout ideas for breaking down these forechecking schemes. Typically at the youth levels, teams will play one of the following penalty-kill forechecks: 1-1-2, 2-2, or 1-2-1.

Penalty-Kill Forecheck: 1-1-2

Variation 1 (figure 14.1*a*): Pressure the first pass. In the first variation of the 1-1-2 penalty-kill forecheck, the first forechecker (F1) starts in the middle of the ice and slowly backs up until a pass is made or is about to be made. He will then angle and attack the player about to receive the pass. The second forechecker (F2) holds the center of the ice.

Variation 2 (figure 14.1*b*): Pressure the puck carrier. In the second variation of the 1-1-2 penalty-kill forecheck, F1 starts in the middle of the ice. As soon as the puck carrier begins carrying the puck up ice, the forechecker angles and attacks the puck carrier, attempting to force him to make a pass. F2 holds the center of the ice until he can determine which direction the pass is going, at which time he attempts to angle and pressure the player about to receive the pass.

The two rear penalty killers line up between the red line and the far blue line, trying not to let anyone behind them.

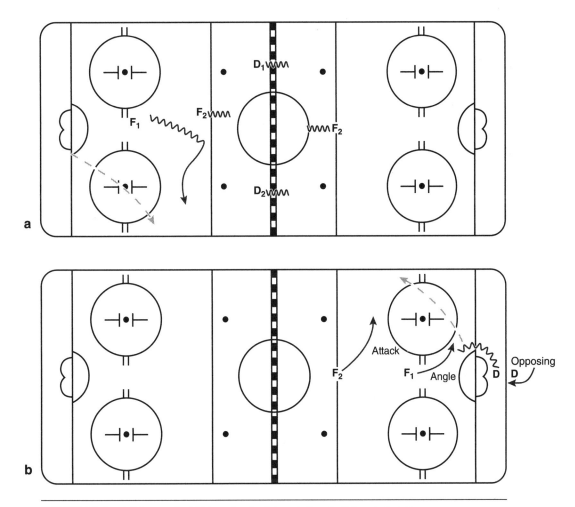

FIGURE 14.1 1-1-2 penalty-kill forecheck: *(a)* variation 1; *(b)* variation 2.

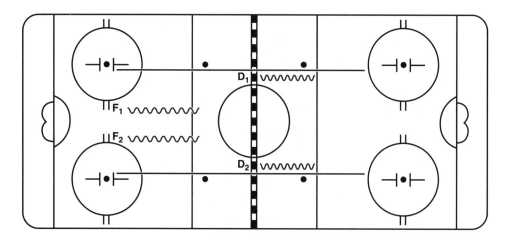

FIGURE 14.2   2-2 penalty-kill forecheck.

Penalty-Kill Forecheck: 2-2

In the 2-2 penalty-kill forecheck (figure 14.2), the penalty-killing team is trying to take away the center of the ice and force the power play to bring the puck up the side of the ice. F1 and F2 will be even or slightly stagger their depth just inside the zone they are forechecking. Instead of pressuring, they simply wait until the power play begins to bring the puck up ice and begin skating backward through the center of the ice, taking away any skating or passing lanes through the center. The two defensemen are also skating a similar pattern behind the two forwards, although their depth will vary depending on the power-play breakout setup, which will be discussed shortly.

Penalty-Kill Forecheck: 1-2-1

In the 1-2-1, or diamond, penalty-kill forecheck (figure 14.3), F1 holds the center of the ice and attempts to force a pass to the side when the puck carrier gets above the top of the circles. At this time, the two players along the wall are prepared to step up or pinch the player about to receive the puck. The rear penalty killer stays back and in the center of the ice, careful not to let anyone behind him. It's the coach's decision how to position the other players. Many coaches favor putting a defenseman on the opposite side of the diamond since they are already used to retrieving pucks and breaking them out when the puck gets dumped. This means there will be a forward on one board and a defenseman on the other. If they are successful in trapping the opponent, the other positions will shift according to figure 14.3.

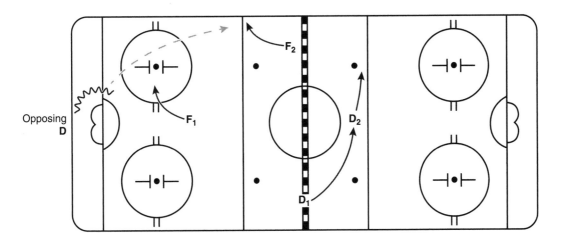

FIGURE 14.3   1-2-1 penalty-kill forecheck.

Breakout Options

Regardless of whether your team is facing any of the three penalty-kill forechecks, the following power-play breakouts can be used to successfully come up the ice if executed properly.

Power-Play Breakout Option 1: Three Back

In figure 14.4, the three players coming back to retrieve the puck should include the two players manning the points once your team gains possession in the offensive zone, as well as one additional player who has the ability to make and receive passes with some level of confidence.

When the penalty-killing unit dumps the puck into your zone, it's important that your three players come back together and with speed. The depth of the two players on the wall swing should be based on the depth of the opponent's forecheck (figure 14.5). For example, if their first forechecker is typically starting around the hash marks, your two players swinging should be close to even to their forecheckers for the best chance at completing the pass.

If the player collecting the puck picks it up at or near the goal line, he has the option of stopping behind the net to wait for the other two players to time their swing. If he can catch the opponent's players in a line change, however, he should break out from behind the net and begin skating up ice, or taking ice. The two swing players will simply open up and support the puck carrier as an outlet.

While the puck is being broken out of the zone, the other two players (typically forwards) will be skating their routes through the neutral zone.

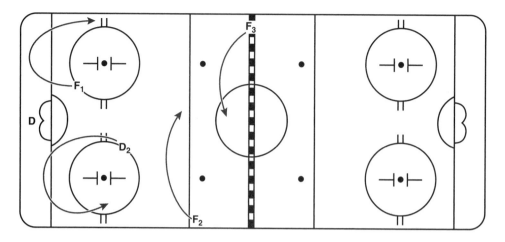

FIGURE 14.4 Three back with one forward on the near blue line and one forward on the red line.

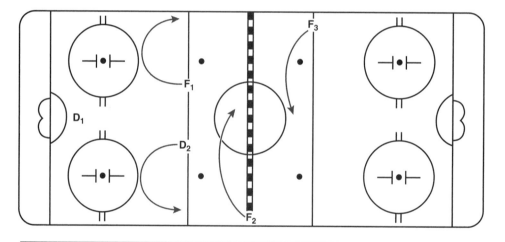

FIGURE 14.5 Three back with the forwards adjusting their swing depth and skating into the zone together.

They typically won't receive the initial pass from the puck carrier but will end up supporting the puck once the initial pass is made (figure 14.6). These players must be extremely diligent in timing their skating patterns through the neutral zone to avoid showing up at the puck too early or too late. Usually these players will want to start skating slowly when the breakout begins, then explode into an area to support the play once that first pass is made.

When the breakout begins and each player skates his route, the goal of the puck carrier is to beat the first forechecker with the initial pass.

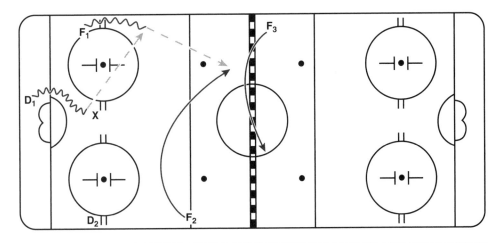

FIGURE 14.6 Three back; puck carrier makes initial pass to player on wall; near forward skates across to support the puck.

The puck carrier has to exercise patience and pass the puck when the first forechecker is beaten or trapped.

If the first forechecker isn't aggressive, the puck carrier should skate the puck at him to freeze him (figure 14.7). Once the first forechecker has been frozen, a pass can be made to a support player, thereby beating the first forechecker.

To beat an aggressive forecheck, the first player back must sprint to the puck, look over his shoulder twice (shoulder check), and trap the first forechecker. If the first forechecker is aggressive and pressuring the puck

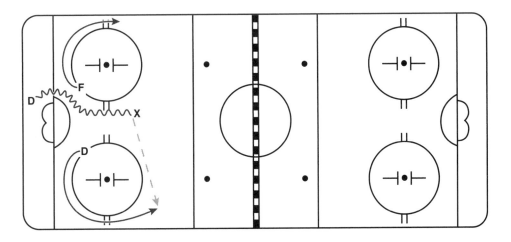

FIGURE 14.7 Three back; first forechecker is passive so puck carrier takes ice, freezes the first forechecker, and dishes the puck to a supporting player.

down below the goal line, the goalie should look to play the puck if the forechecker might win the race to the puck. In this scenario, where your players get beaten to the puck, the first player back should open up and present a passing option for the goaltender (figure 14.8).

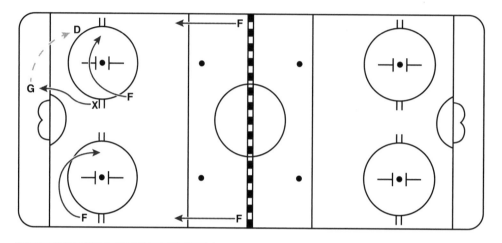

FIGURE 14.8   Three back; first forechecker comes hard and beats the defense back; defense opens up and receives a pass from the goalie.

Power-Play Breakout Option 2: Five Back

In this scheme, all five players on the ice come back to assist in the break-out. It is the coach's responsibility to determine the exact position each player will fill on the power-play breakout. At Denver, when we posted our power-play lineups, we also posted a breakout formation to ensure the players know exactly where they were supposed to be during a breakout. Figure 14.9 shows an example of a power-play breakout lineup from the 2008-2009 season.

This power-play breakout is similar to the three-back breakout discussed earlier. However, two additional support players are added just inside of the players on the wall. This allows the puck carrier to make a shorter first pass while also giving the inside player the option to skate the puck, make a short pass to the outside support player, or make a short pass back to the original puck carrier (figure 14.10).

Once again, the timing of the players coming back into the zone and coming up the ice together is critical to ensure the maximum number of options on the power-play breakout. Several factors go into identifying the best position for a player on the power-play breakout:

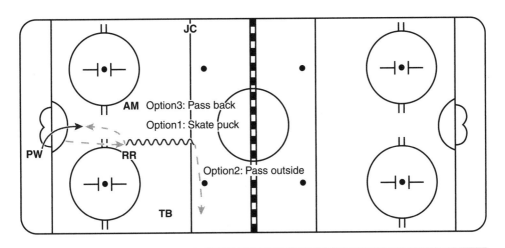

FIGURE 14.9 Five back with player initials.

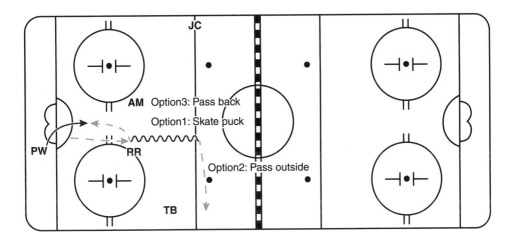

FIGURE 14.10 Five-back options once puck is moved to inside player.

1. The location of the player in the offensive zone, once zone entry is gained
2. The player's shooting side, right or left
3. The player's endurance level

Let's look at each of these. In any power-play offensive zone setup, typically two players will be on the point and three will be stationed lower in the zone. At least two of the players stationed lower in the zone should be the higher swing players on the breakout to conserve their energy and prevent them from having to come back the full length of the ice (figure 14.11).

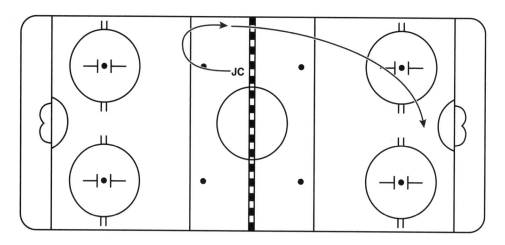

FIGURE 14.11 Five back; path of high swing player to his respective spot in the offensive zone.

One potential issue with all five players coming back for the power-play breakout is that several may be on their backhand coming up the ice. Although this may not be an issue for older athletes, younger kids may struggle with backhand passes. There is no right or wrong solution to this problem, but it is something to be aware of when you're developing your power-play breakout. Remember the discussion earlier in the chapter that mentioned breaking down systems into smaller, simpler skills. In this case, it is receiving a pass on a backhand. If your system has players coming up the ice on their backhands, be sure to run practice drills in which these players work specifically on this skill, and not just when practicing the power-play breakout.

Another factor to consider when determining a player's location on the swing is his endurance level. Players who tend to have less endurance should be higher swing players to prevent them from coming back the full length of the ice. Since these suggestions are merely guidelines, feel free to adjust the breakout to suit the needs of your team.

Similar to breaking out against a 1-1-2 forecheck, the puck carrier should attempt to skate the puck until he is pressured by the first forechecker. At that time, the puck carrier should pass to one of the inside swing players, effectively trapping the first forechecker. After making the pass, it is important for the initial puck carrier to continue supporting the play, without putting himself even with the new puck carrier.

The new puck carrier may or may not have time and space to continue skating the puck. However, he should have support from the wide player, usually within 10 feet, if he receives pressure from a second forechecker.

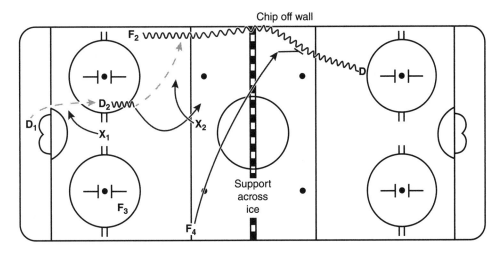

FIGURE 14.12 Five back; two on one with two swing players against the second forechecker near the wall.

It is imperative that the new puck carrier exercise patience and look to create a new two on one against the second forechecker (figure 14.12).

Now that the puck is being advanced up one side of the ice, the inside swing player from the opposite side of the ice, in an attempt to outnumber the penalty killers, should start skating across in order to create another support option. The neutral zone will become crowded with players very quickly, potentially making it difficult to make a perfect tape-to-tape pass. Another option for the puck carrier is to make an area pass to a space behind the penalty killers and allow the forwards to skate into it. With the crackdown on obstruction and holding, this has become a very popular strategy in today's game.

One common mistake made during the power-play breakout is for players to skate to their respective spots in the offensive zone before the team has clear possession. This typically results in a one-on-one or two-on-two battle for the puck, with the penalty killers clearing the puck the length of the ice. Coaches must continue to emphasize outnumbering the opponent in every loose puck battle, or scrum, until the team has clear possession of the puck. At that time, players can begin to rotate into their correct power-play positions.

Practicing the Power-Play Breakout

There are several ways to practice the power-play breakout. As discussed earlier, one of the most important aspects of the breakout is timing. Practice and repetition are required to perfect the timing of the breakout. The simplest way to practice the power-play breakout is to have the players break the puck out without any pressure at all from the penalty-kill forecheck. This will enable the members of the power play to familiarize themselves with their positions and their roles without having to initially worry about pressure from the penalty killers.

Team Drill 1: Progressive Penalty Killers

Power-play players start on the far blue line. The coach stands at center ice with the puck. The coach dumps the puck, and the players move to their breakout positions and start the breakout (figure 14.13). The coach can pressure initially. The progression is to add two, three, and then four penalty killers. Once the power play has entered the offensive zone, the coach blows the whistle and throws a new puck back into the breakout zone, and the players do it again. The original puck is dead at this point. Give the first power-play group approximately two or three repetitions before switching to the next group.

If your team has only half ice during practice, power-play players can start on the red line instead of the far blue line for this drill.

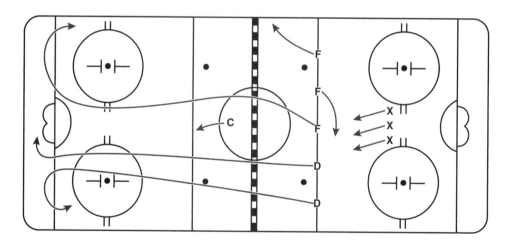

FIGURE 14.13 Team drill 1: progressive penalty killers.

Team Drill 2: Breakout

Players start in their offensive zone setup against the penalty kill. Players move the puck for approximately 10 seconds, and then the coach blows the whistle. Once the whistle sounds, the coach throws a puck into the defensive zone, and the power-play unit has to skate back into the zone into breakout position (figure 14.14). The penalty killers then start their forechecks. The drill should run for 40 seconds total, including the 10 seconds to start the drill in the offensive zone. If the power play breaks the puck out easily and gains zone entry, the coach should blow the whistle and throw a new puck back into the defensive zone for them to start again.

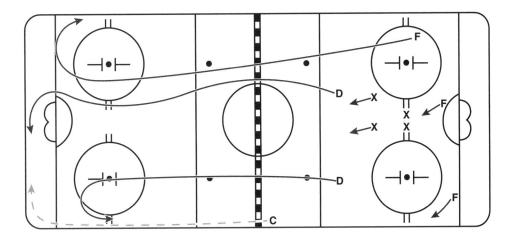

FIGURE 14.14   Team drill 2: breakout.

Individual Drill 1: Defensemen

This is a defenseman-oriented drill. Defenders collect the puck behind the net, move it to their forehands, and either use the net or counter before passing to a player on the wall (figure 14.15).

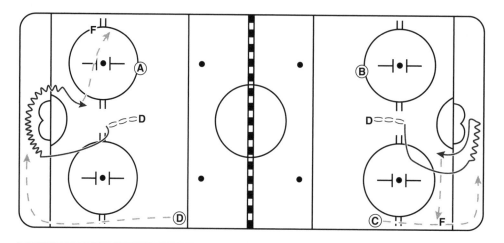

FIGURE 14.15 Individual drill 1: defensemen.

Individual Drill 2: Four-Dot Chip Drill

The four-dot chip drill will help players get used to supporting the puck and chipping past forecheckers in the neutral zone. For the four dots, you can use players, coaches, or cones (figure 14.16). Two players start at opposite sides on one end of the ice. The far player skates toward the puck carrier on the other side and receives the puck. She makes a chip pass off the boards that is retrieved by her partner. They continue up the ice, chipping the puck off the boards and skating around the dots, until they reach the other end of the ice. The player with the puck finishes by taking a shot at the net.

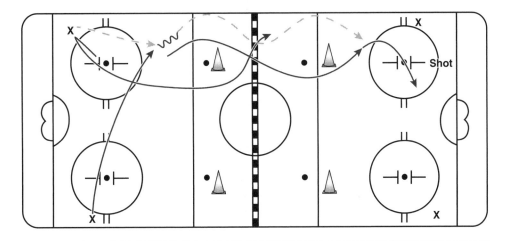

FIGURE 14.16   Individual drill 2: four-dot chip drill.

POWER PLAY: IN-ZONE SETUP

Once your breakout has successfully gained possession in the offensive zone, there are several options for getting scoring chances and scoring goals.

Based on a team's personnel and each player's strengths, each offensive zone setup will vary slightly. However, several guidelines apply regardless of the power-play setup or the type of penalty kill you're facing:

- ◆ Don't pass up shots from the house (figure 14.17).
- ◆ The puck carrier must work to find shooting lanes, either by skating the puck or working a give-and-go with a teammate.
- ◆ When the puck is in the house, there should be at least one player at the front of the net screening the goalie, facing the puck, and looking for tips or deflections.
- ◆ Once the puck is shot on net, two or three players should be crashing the net or slot area for rebounds.

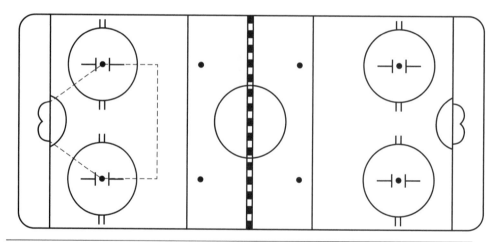

FIGURE 14.17 The house.

Power-Play Setup Option 1

In figure 14.18, both players on the point are on their one-time sides, which means the right-handed player is playing on the left point and the left-handed player is playing on the right point. This is beneficial for several reasons. For one, it allows them to skate the puck toward the middle of the ice more easily because they can push it on their forehand.

In addition, they can one-time a pass from the other point or a player on the other side board more easily (figure 14.19).

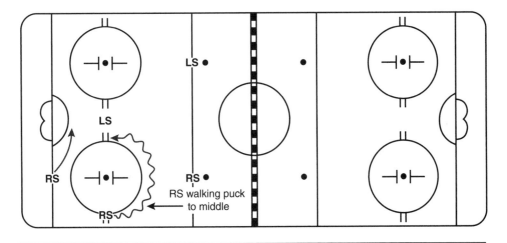

FIGURE 14.18   Right shot walking puck toward middle of ice for shot.

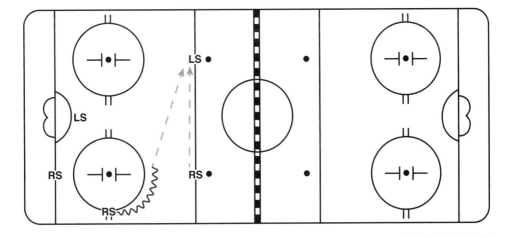

FIGURE 14.19   Left shot receiving one-time pass from his partner and the opposite side board for a shot.

The other three players stationed lower in the zone are also intentionally on the correct sides based on whether they are right or left shots. The two right shots have multiple options between the two of them to generate scoring chances:

- They can work a give-and-go (figure 14.20*a*).

- They can walk the seam for a shot on net. When the player along the boards begins walking this seam, the other player should begin skating toward the net for a rebound.

- They can pass from the side board to the goal line and attack the net for a stuff attempt. When the player below the goal line tries to stuff the puck in the net, the other player immediately skates toward the net for a rebound.

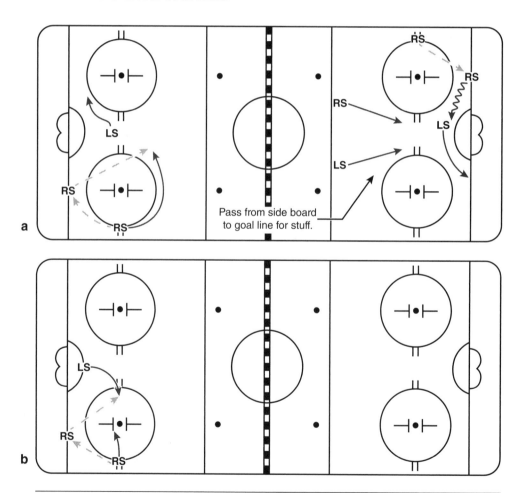

FIGURE 14.20 Options for the two right shots to score: *(a)* give-and-go; *(b)* net-front left shot.

◆ They can use the net-front left shot as a pop-out option (figure 14.20*b*). Both right-handed players should begin skating toward the net for a rebound.

Obviously this type of formation can work on both sides of the ice, depending on your personnel.

Power-Play Setup Option 2

The setup shown in figure 14.21 is sometimes called an umbrella setup because the formation looks similar to an umbrella when the players are in the correct positions. Up top near the blue line is one player in the center of the ice. On either side of him, but closer to the boards and near the tops of the circles, are two other players. In front of the net is either one or two players, depending on your choice of setup. The last player might instead position himself off to the side in the side-slot area or closer to the goal line.

The power play typically cannot enter the umbrella setup as soon as they enter the zone. Once the power-play unit has clear puck possession in the offensive zone, they should work the puck up to the defenseman you have selected to walk the puck to the middle of the ice. As the defenseman starts walking the puck, the other player on the point repositions himself near the top of the circle while facing and staying open to the puck, just in case the point gets pressured and a quick pass has to be made to the side boards.

One of the low forwards along the wall also has to come up toward the top of the circle as the defenseman starts moving across the middle. The defenseman may also use this player as a passing option, depending

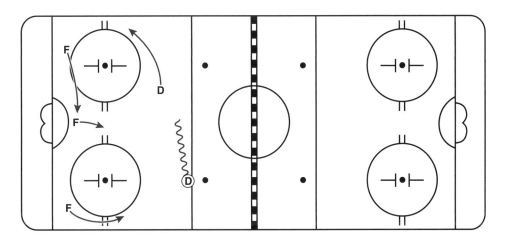

FIGURE 14.21 Umbrella setup.

on where the pressure is coming from. One of the goals of the umbrella formation is to get the puck to the top of the umbrella for a point shot with an open shooting lane and a player screening the goalie at the front of the net.

To create this shooting lane, the power-play unit has to create a two-on-one against the penalty killer up top and catch him out of position. Depending on the penalty kill, this may be accomplished by having the point man pass the puck down to the player on the wall and then having the player on the wall pass the puck right back to the point, where the player has already opened up for a one-time shot (figure 14.22).

The players down low have the responsibility to screen the goalie and also look for tips when the shot is taken. To accomplish either of these tasks, they must battle against the penalty-killing defensemen in front of the net to gain body positioning closer to the puck without getting boxed out. Typically, penalty-killing defensemen are taught to either box out or front and block once the shot is taken from the point. Boxing out is accomplished by physically pushing any players from the net-front area. Fronting and blocking requires a penalty-killing defenseman to get on the puck side of the player screening the goalie and attempt to block the shot once it is taken. Either way, the power-play forwards at the front of the net are constantly fighting for body positioning and space on the ice in front of the goalie. Their goal is to position themselves outside of the crease area, with the backs of their heels just above the paint of the crease. Johan Franzen has mastered this skill for the Detroit Red Wings.

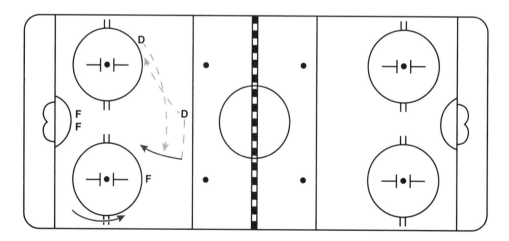

FIGURE 14.22 The point man passes to the player on the wall and then skates backward to open up for a shot. The forward on the wall one-touches back to the point, catching the penalty killer out of position.

Practicing the Power Play in Zone

Similar to practicing the power-play breakout, practicing the power play in zone is best done initially without pressure. This skeleton setup allows the players to get used to making hard tape-to-tape passes without having to initially worry about the pass being intercepted or tipped by a penalty killer. In addition, the coach can call out certain sequences to get the players used to different options that may be available during the game.

Like any other small game in practice, attempt to create competition in these power-play drills. You can either have the power play compete against the penalty kill or create two teams, with each team having to play both roles. The important point is to keep score, regardless of how you choose to score the game in the following drills. One example can be to award the penalty kill a point if they clear the puck from the defensive zone, while the power play gets a point for a shot on net.

Team Drill 1: End Zone Game

Set up two different power-play units at both ends (figure 14.23). When one penalty kill clears the puck, the other end begins. This game can be played 4v3, 5v3, or 5v4. It should begin from a face-off in order to teach the power-play unit face-off intensity and competitiveness.

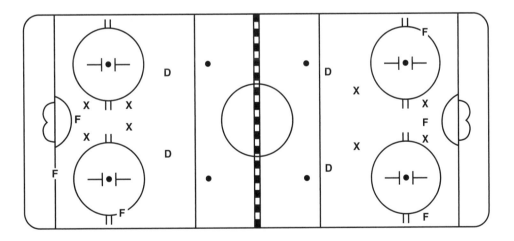

FIGURE 14.23   Team drill 1: end zone game.

Team Drill 2: Full-Ice Game

Play the power play versus the penalty kill on either full ice or half ice, depending on what you have. The drill should start from a face-off in the offensive zone (figure 14.24) and continue for 40 seconds. If a goal is scored, the coach gives a new puck to the power-play unit. If the penalty killers clear the puck, the power-play unit has to break it out and the penalty-killers begin forechecking.

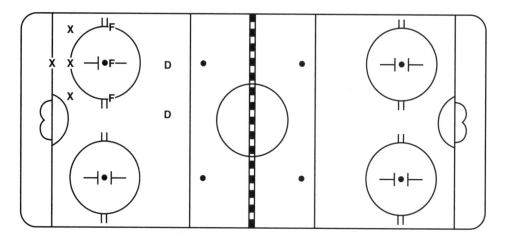

FIGURE 14.24 Team drill 2: full-ice game.

Team Drill 3: Appert Pro Set 3v2 Drill

There is an imaginary line down the middle of the ice that cannot be crossed (figure 14.25). This simulates a three on two in the power-play offensive zone against two penalty killers. If the puck crosses the imaginary line, the next group plays it live. If the puck is cleared, the coach throws in a new puck.

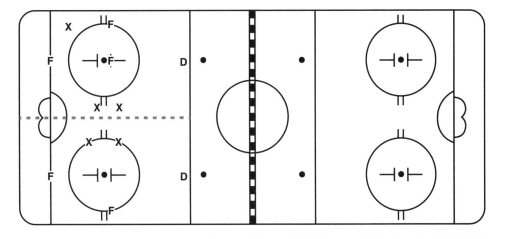

FIGURE 14.25   Team drill 3: Appert pro set 3v2 drill.

Individual Drill 1: Defenders

The coach works with the defenders to keep the puck in at the point, both on forehand and backhand. Defenders take a few steps and shoot (figure 14.26).

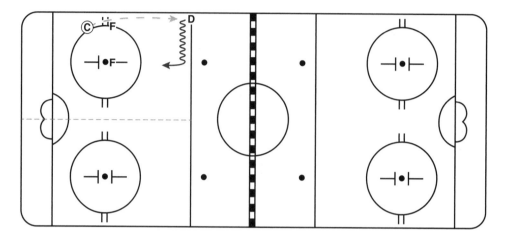

FIGURE 14.26   Individual drill 1: defenders.

Individual Drill 2:
Game-Day Shooting With Defenders

Two coaches on the side boards pass pucks hard or indirectly to defenders (figure 14.27). Players keep the puck in, then pass the first one. The second one they receive and then pass and shoot.

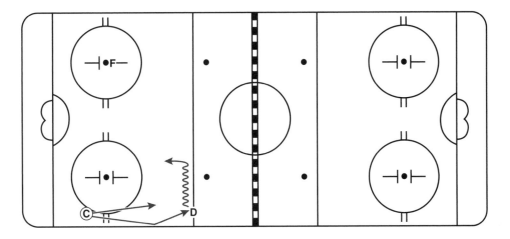

FIGURE 14.27   Individual drill 2: game-day shooting with defenders.

Individual Drill 3: Forwards

The coach works with the forwards on the side boards to pick up rimmed pucks along the wall and walk the seam (figure 14.28).

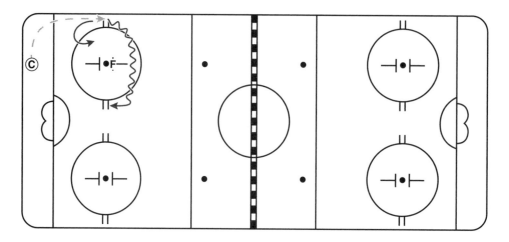

FIGURE 14.28 Individual drill 3: forwards.

Individual Drill 4: Low Forwards

The coach works with the low forwards to attack the net from the goal line (figure 14.29).

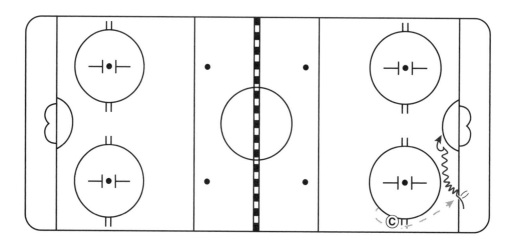

FIGURE 14.29 Individual drill 4: low forwards.

CONCLUSION

Special teams, including the power play, have become an important part of any successful hockey team. Time spent developing these plays and drilling them is time spent well. Successful special teams require team coordination and individual skill and effort. A coach should evaluate his players and create a unit of five players who complement each other's strengths and weaknesses.

For power-play breakouts, simple is often better. Take advantage of the unequal numbers on the ice to create two-on-one situations. Develop breakouts in consideration of your opponent's penalty-kill forechecks. Common penalty-kill forechecks at the youth hockey level include the 1-1-2, the 2-2, and the 1-2-1. Options such as three back and five back can be used to overcome penalty-kill forechecks.

Once the breakout successfully moves the puck into the offensive zone, the power-play team regroups to take advantage of their position and score goals. Regardless of the team's strategy, the power-play team must always take shots from the house, find the shooting lanes, screen the goalie, and crash the net for rebounds. Two setup options include the umbrella setup and another in which a right-handed player is playing the left point and a left-handed player is playing the right point.

Both team and individual drills are necessary to develop special teams skills and prepare players for taking advantage of these situations. Drills can feature a competitive element to increase player interest and create more gamelike situations. Teams that practice hard and plan well will be in the best position to use power plays to their advantage.

15

Scouting Opponents

Nate Leaman

At the college level, scouting opponents is accepted as a basic component of game preparation. Although there are some opportunities for a staff member attending a game to do this live,* more often than not scouting is accomplished through breaking down video of the opponent shared through league or national policy. The advantage of watching an opponent live is that you can get a better feel for their game, as well as a view of the complete ice. But at the college level, schedules, geography, and NCAA rules combine to limit those opportunities.

When scouting opponents, the critical factor is to distinguish between what the players need to know versus what the coaches need to know. There is a legitimate concern that giving the players too much information about an opponent will detract from their first responsibility, which is to focus on what they do well. Too much information can paralyze your players.

Preparation breeds confidence. Coaches must know the opponent's strengths, be ready to attack the opponent's weaknesses, and be prepared for all situations that may occur during the game. This level of preparation often takes more than one scouting opportunity. Watching the last game a team played may not prepare you for what you will see come game time. Teams at the collegiate level make adjustments every game, and different adjustments for different opponents, so it's best to review several tapes of your opponent, including your last game against this team.

Of course, coaches want to be prepared, but we don't want to create tension or put our players on their heels by overadjusting and focusing too much on the opponent. Always let your players know what you want them to attack, but never take away from what your team does well. This has a significant impact on your team's confidence. Building up your opponent

---

* In January 2013, the NCAA passed new legislation prohibiting coaches from live scouting of opponents unless teams are competing in the same event.

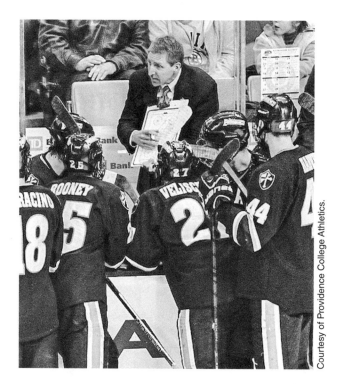

Courtesy of Providence College Athletics.

(or the game itself) too much can result in your team playing emotionally tight, waiting for the opponent to act. Your players won't have the same energy needed to perform their tasks. Hockey is a read and react game, and your primary focus is to enable your team to react to situations they see in the game and play on their toes.

Normally, this amount of scouting detail requires roughly three hours of dissecting each game film and taking notes. We often watch multiple games of the team we're scouting to get an accurate read. How hard you want to prepare for your opponent is an individual decision for each coach, but the key is providing your team with the adjustments they need to know that won't take them out of their style of game.

Our staff will watch game film on our upcoming opponent on Sunday or Monday so we can properly discuss and map out any adjustments we'd like to make in our game and how we'll teach the adjustments to the team during upcoming practices. For example, we may have scouted an opponent and realized that one of their strengths is they generate much of their offense through a very aggressive forecheck. As a result, we'll break down the forecheck to determine what their players are doing (sending one man at the D, two men at both D, pinch on the walls, and so on).

Second, we want to know how they generate scoring chances from their forecheck. Our coaches need to know this information going into the game. We'll discuss several ways to break out the puck, taking away our opponent's strength. Last, we'll discuss how to teach the players our new breakout techniques, and how we'll incorporate those breakout techniques into our drills that week. Again, note the evolution from what the coaches have scouted to the final product taught to the players. Coaches need to teach the players how to react.

During a video review on Wednesday (after discussing the adjustments with the team and doing drills), we may show several clips of the forecheck and then a couple of clips of what we believe will beat that forecheck. The video helps the players visualize the adjustments and what they'll see in the game. In practice on Wednesday and Thursday, we'll continue to cover what *we* want to do. In our scouting report to the players (see figure 15.1 for an example), we'll also cover the actions we want players to execute. As coaches, we understand what the opponent is doing, but the coaches must keep the players focused on what they need to execute.

WEEKLY SCHEDULE

For the most part, our schedule is set up so we practice Monday through Thursday, play games on the weekend, and give the players a day off on Sunday. Roughly, this is how we use that time.

On Sunday or Monday, we implement a strategy for Tuesday, Wednesday, and Thursday practices. The staff review scouting films on the next opponent. We also review our postgame notes from previous games against the upcoming opponent. These could be from a previous year—coaches definitely have tendencies—or they could be from earlier the same season. The latter is more relevant, as it involves the same team we are about to play. The staff also reviews key stats on the opponent including the following:

- Scoring leaders and shot leaders
- Breakdown of goals
- Special teams versus even strength
- Goaltending
- Scoring by periods (trends early and late in games)
- Penalty minutes per game
- Lineup over last two games (a loaded top line and defensive pair or a more balanced lineup)
- Points by defensemen
- Best face-off men
- Best and worst plus–minus players

Providence College vs. Mankato State

Be quietly focused, and play a great positional game. Play with poise and look to make plays on the ice. Execution over emotion. A great deal of our offense will come from good defense. We need to be disciplined and not allow their PP.

1. They are a good transition/rush team and love to use their defenseman on the rush and in their OZP.
- Strong plays attacking the zone, in the OZ, and in the danger areas! Make them play D by getting pucks behind their defenseman and owning the lane to get our OZP going. Keep a good high F3 in our OZP.
- Fs help our D by coming back hard through the center of the OBL. Find their 3rd and 4th men in the rush and be D-side. Tight gaps by our D giving no space; talk and point so we communicate. Four or five players back to blow up their rush offense.
- Eliminate men jumping into the offense by finishing hits on their D and Fs on the FC and NZD.

2. OZP they like to chip to back of net and center pucks. Their D are very active with high rolls and coming down to the net backdoor.
- Anticipate chips to the back of the net. Meet the puck there and be physical. If you are late, lead with stick on puck.
- D finish the shooter/passer and stay D-side of their men away from the puck.
- Wings keep your head on a swivel and stay D side of their D.

3. Work their D down low by protecting the puck. Get our bodies over the puck while moving our feet. Use cutbacks to create space. Chip pucks on first touch when you feel pressure and beat men off the puck. The goal is to get men and pucks to the net. Penetrate the house and generate second and third chances.

Notes

PP IZ: Like to move the puck from half wall to below the goalline and look for pass-outs to men off the near and far posts from behind the net.

F/Os: DZ wins go to the weakside wing. Get into them as they want to get up and go, especially off a DZ win or a NZ win.

OZ: On wins back to point, look for inside or boardside winger to come high with D. Our D must follow him up and close the gap.

FC: One man, D look to use the net or your partner on breakouts.
7 Palmquist and **18 Leitner** are their top players we need to finish our hits against them.

35 Williams struggles holding pucks. We need to get to the net away from the puck and throw pucks at him from all angles.

Top Players

12 Lafontaine

18 Leitner

7 Palmquist

Goaltending

35 Williams .924

FIGURE 15.1 Sample scouting report.

On Tuesday, we may begin to implement some adjustments we have in mind for that weekend's opponent(s). It may be two or three things that we adjust. For example, how are we planning to break the puck out against a particular opponent? Or it could be more substantial. Adjustments are almost always made to our special teams. Since we work on power play and penalty killing every day in practice, these adjustments will be made beginning Tuesdays.

On Wednesday, we present a short video (two to three minutes) that covers what we want the team to know about our opponent, including special teams. This is not a time-consuming endeavor. As mentioned previously, we don't want to overwhelm the players or have them thinking too much about the opponent. What the coaches know will be very different from what the players know.

On Thursday, we share our scouting report with the team. It's important to note that these scouting reports are more about what *we* want to do, not so much about the opponent's tendencies. These are two or three items, offensively and defensively, that we need to be prepared for and how we want to play, including face-offs, key players, and special teams.

On Friday we have a team meeting to go over key points in each zone.

FILM BREAKDOWN

When the staff breaks down the game film, we look at opponent's tendencies in each zone.

In the defensive zone:

- Do they keep a D at net front? Is their D zone coverage man to man or zone?
- In D zone coverage, what do wings do? Collapse, lock off the walls, or play man to man?
- In D zone coverage, will they outnumber around the puck (commit three men and flood the puck)?
- How do they break out under pressure versus no pressure (weak-side or strong-side breakout)?
- Do they have three right-shot D and three left-shot?
- Do they jump D on breakouts?
- What are their offensive and defensive tendencies?
- Does the strong-side or weak-side defenseman retrieve the puck on dump-ins?
- How do they play a two-on-one rush?

In the neutral zone:

- Is their first forward passive or aggressive?
- What is open: strong side, weak side, or middle?
- Does the opponent's D step up?
- Offensively, do they like to go D to D or north–south up the ice?
- Do they like to use their strong side, weak side, or middle?

In the offensive zone:

- What forechecking system or scheme do they use?
- Do they tend to dump in or carry in for possession?
- Are they a cycle team or a quick-strike, throw the puck at the net team?
- Are their defensemen active?
- Are they a one-on-one team?

We then look at special teams and other areas.

On the power play:

- Who is their most dangerous player? Their weakest player?
- How do they play their defensemen? Off hand, narrow, wide, or strong side?
- What are their priority plays?
- What is their breakout? Who do they want to get the puck to?
- What lines do they use after the power play expires?

On the penalty kill:

- Do they use an aggressive or passive forecheck?
- Do they have different systems with different forwards on the ice?
- Do they angle down with top forwards on the ice?
- What is the rotation of their forwards (best players to worst)?
- What lines do they use after the penalty kill expires?

Regarding goaltending:

- How is the goaltender's rebound control? The positioning of his hands and feet? Where has he been beaten before?
- How much does the goaltender like to play the puck?
- What are the goaltender's positioning habits (deep or aggressive)?
- What is the goaltender's temperament?

We examine their face-off plays in the offensive zone, neutral zone, and defensive zone. Here are some specific elements on face-offs:

- Do the opposing centers try to win the face-off with their sticks, or do they get their bodies involved? Do they spin and win with their feet?
- Who is the opponent's top center on face-offs, and what does he like to do? Go to forehand or backhand?
- Which players forecheck off of offensive zone and neutral zone face-off losses?
- What face-off plays do they run in the offensive zone and neutral zone?
- How do the opponents break the puck out of face-off wins in the defensive zone?

We examine the opponent's top players and their tendencies:

- Do they have any top offensive defensemen who like to jump into the offense with any regularity or come to the net during offensive play?
- What are the tendencies of their top forwards? Cutbacks? Certain rush moves?
- Do they have any big physical players whom we might be better *not* establishing contact with because we will not win these situations?

Regarding game considerations:

- Which matchups appear to be in our favor?
- What type of game do we expect, a grinding defensive battle or a high-paced game?
- What is the opponent's coaching style? Do they match lines?
- What lines does the opposing coach use after power play and penalty kill?
- Who are the referees, and what are their tendencies?
- What are the characteristics of the rink (road games)?
- What type of crowd atmosphere do we anticipate?

CONCLUSION

This chapter lists many things to look for when scouting opponents, but after watching all the tape, be sure to limit the gathered information and focus only on the items or adjustments you believe will be pertinent to winning the game.

Finally, although they were mentioned only briefly in the chapter, post-game notes are an underappreciated part of the scouting process. Right after the game, and again after watching the film, you have your best education on what was successful against an opponent, what areas of the game you struggled with, and the opposing coach's tendencies. Typing up detailed notes and filing them for later review can be some of your best preparation for later games against the same opponent.

16

International Play

Mike Eaves

What truly differentiates international competition from North American play is the size of the ice surface. The Olympic ice is 200 feet long by 100 feet wide, as opposed to the NHL's ice surface of 200 feet long by only 85 feet wide. The additional width puts a premium on the skills of the game. Skating, puck handling, and passing are required skills in order to be successful on this larger sheet of ice.

The North American game has the added element of body contact, which is as necessary as the previously mentioned skills. In the late 1970s and early 1980s, it wasn't uncommon to hear European fans say they enjoyed the North American style of play because of the physical contact. When Europeans first came to play in North America, they weren't ready for this physical element, and as a result a lot of early skilled Europeans returned home.

This is not as often the case anymore, as Europeans now have NHL-size rinks in their homelands to practice and prepare for the physical rigors of the North American game. In addition, the European professionals who currently play in North America are returning to their homelands to teach and counsel younger players on how to play a more North American game. The net result is a great blend of skill combined with a physical element.

Because of the emphasis on skill in the international game, North Americans have to adjust their aggressive style of play, since international officials tend to call the game closer to the letter of the law. If North American teams don't come to terms with this fact, they'll find themselves being very frustrated and spending time in the penalty box. From there, they will be looking at some of the best power plays in the world. It's not a good position to be in. Teams need to understand this and would benefit from having an official at practice calling penalties in a scrimmage situation to help players understand firsthand what they can expect to experience in international play.

Courtesy of University of Wisconsin Athletic Communications.

One of the unique aspects of international hockey is the development of young players. From the very beginning, young players work on the skills of the game. The emphasis is on skating, puck handling, and passing. The only games these young people play are small-area games (1v1, 2v2, 3v3). We all marvel at the skill set of the European players. What are their secrets? How do they develop such marvelous skill with their players?

Years back, we had an opportunity to play in a Five Nations Tournament in Siberia with an under-18 team. During the tournament, we were able to observe practices of 10- to 12-year-old players. In a 90-minute span, they spent 45 minutes practicing skating skills and the other 45 minutes working on the combination of puck handling and passing. They didn't scrimmage. They did not, on this particular day, even play a small-area game. Their secret is simple: They practice the right things. They build from the ground up. The idea is to get the skills, apply the skills in small-area games, and then apply those skills in game situations. Their practice-to-game ratio as they grow older is still 3-to-1.

In North America we primarily take the exact opposite route. We play games and tournaments and then more games and tournaments. What we get is the odd child who stands out because of natural ability and a group of others who do the best they can and usually end up body-checking everything in sight because they have little skill. What we do very well is compete. The international game has learned, and can continue to learn, from us in this aspect of the game. We can learn about the development of skill from our counterparts in Europe. Let's find that balance of developing skill first before putting our kids in game situations.

Most international teams adopt a particular style of play. They use it in all national teams, starting at junior ages (15 to 20). During the European professional season, they take breaks around Thanksgiving and at Christmas to bring their national team players together. They practice and play some games to get ready for international competition, whether it is the Olympics or the world championships. The benefit of this is that although they may play on other teams, they know that when playing for their country, they play a certain style.

All combined, the European countries have about 70 training days together as a team during the course of a year. The North American teams may get 14 days, if they're fortunate, before an international tournament. This is a huge advantage for the European teams when they play against North American teams. Until recently, through the National Team Development Program (NTDP), the United States would put good players together and hope they would gel quickly and win. Taking good players who are on the same page system-wise makes for a far superior team. History proves this.

Let's look at some countries around the world that compete at a high level, how they play, and my insights from personal experience.

CANADA

Courtesy of USA Hockey/Jeff Cable.

The Canadians hold the sport of ice hockey near and dear to their hearts. Nowhere in the world does one sport define a country like hockey defines Canada. The lead stories in all aspects of sports media revolve around the

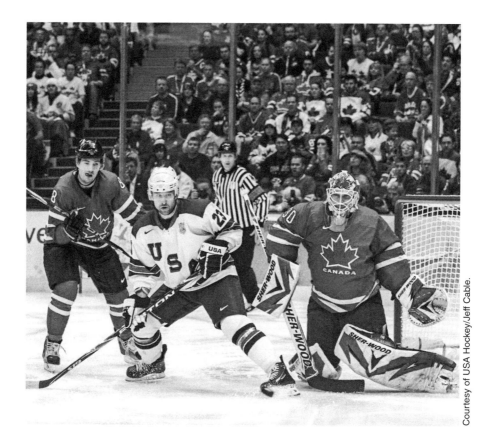

world of hockey. It is what gives this country a huge part of its national identity and pride.

Their style is basic and direct. They play aggressively in all aspects of the game, with speed, and with some of the most talented players in the world. Compared to European countries, they will make more body contact and shoot the puck more often. Their teams are usually big. The coaching is highly dedicated to all aspects of the game, but the basic premise is, "If you are going to win, you will have to take it away from us." Canada may not have the highest pure skill level compared with other countries, but their ability to play with heart and soul is an intangible they bring to the rink every time they play.

Canada as a country is fine-tuning its system of developing talent. Like the United States, there is still too much emphasis on games and not enough on skill development. It is a societal issue, as parents want their kids to play games rather than practice to develop skill. Nevertheless, many of this country's best athletes migrate to hockey. As a result, and with the coaching knowledge and passion for the game, Canada always competes at the highest levels.

CZECH REPUBLIC

The Czechs, like those in most European countries, do a great job of developing skill. They have terrific stick skills and produce a high number of goal scorers, Jaromir Jagr being one of them. Their national teams always seem to have big players. Their defensemen consistently range from six foot one to six foot three. They have developed a system to produce skilled goalies as well.

Their national system of play is based more on control. They like to use a 1-2-2 system that gets the opponent into tighter spaces. They want to create turnovers and counter as quickly as possible. Part of the counter is to have their first forechecker stretch after his forechecking effort. Their power play revolves around the umbrella setup.

The Czechs are well coached and will adapt to an opponent's tactics during the course of the game. They are excellent at drawing penalties. They have confidence in their abilities. At times in world competition they have been brilliant, and then they can be average, depending on how things are going.

SWEDEN

Since adopting the game, the Swedes have been among the most skilled hockey players in the world. They do an intelligent job of off-ice and on-ice training. Off ice, they work the different age groups appropriately in terms of training. On ice, they focus on the correct areas and keep their practice-to-game ratios at an optimum proportion.

Physically, the Swedes traditionally have tall men playing on their national teams, sprinkled in with skilled and dynamic smaller forwards. (The first Swede to score 50 goals in the NHL was Calgary Flame Hakan Loob, who was only five feet, nine inches tall and 176 pounds.)

In my experience, one of the most unique aspects of Swedish hockey is how social they are about the game. Before games, they like to gather and review the game plan together. Whether it is a face-off play, forecheck schemes, or a neutral zone regroup, they love to gather in units, such as defensive pairs or a forward line, to review what the plan is for that particular game.

The Swedish style of play resembles most European teams. They look to control the puck and try to spread out their opponents, and then attack with speed. Without the puck, they are intelligent, using their positioning to force their opponents into smaller spaces (usually in a 1-2-2), looking to create a turnover before counterattacking quickly.

One area of the game in which the Swedes have really improved is their compete level, or intensity during games. Their ability to skate, pass, shoot, and handle the puck has typically been as good as any country in the world. But there came a point after the 2004 World Junior Championship that they took a hard look at their game and what could improve.

The area they felt could improve was the compete level. That incorporates battling for 50-50 pucks, getting better body position in front of the net both offensively and defensively, racing for the puck, and finishing checks. Their international success has improved dramatically since 2004, and that's been a direct result of looking at their game honestly and addressing their needs.

FINLAND

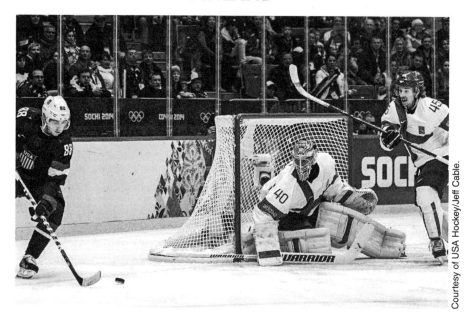

Courtesy of USA Hockey/Jeff Cable.

For a country of roughly five million people, Finland always competes for medals at world events regardless of age level. They do a terrific job of building skill at a young age. The Finns have qualified coaches who must pass certification programs before they are allowed to coach, and then they are hired by professional teams to work with kids in their organizations. If they do a good job, they are hired back at a higher level or they are released.

Finland does a terrific job in dryland training for their young players as well. When they become teenagers, they start learning Olympic lifts just using their hockey sticks. They work on balance and technique at this age. As they get older, they start to use some weight and gradually build to full-time strength training and conditioning.

The Finns are tough competitors. Pound for pound, they may be as tough as any players around the world. It could be that they are survivors, as they have been ruled by both Sweden and Russia. They will compete to the very end of any game and will never give up. They constantly display this trait in their style of play. They like to use the pick play when they have the puck and will initiate body contact when competing for a 50-50 puck.

Another characteristic of the Finns is their ability to produce world-class goalies. Again, they get the right people to work with their young goalies to develop good habits and proper technique.

As a country, their style of play is very distinct. They utilize a 1-1-3 system. How aggressive they are with a system depends on the score, but it is still primarily based on keeping three players back so as not to surrender any odd-man rushes. They usually designate the center to be the third forward back. Their power-play units look very similar, as they like to roll a forward high off the side wall and run the attack from that position. They play and teach the same system to all their national teams so that when they come together, they've already practiced this system over a long period of time. This fact, combined with the way they train and develop skill, makes them a formidable opponent every time.

RUSSIA

You'd be hard pressed to find a hockey insider who would not agree that Russia produces more than its fair share of highly skilled hockey players. The Russians' ability to perform with great skill at top speed is fun to watch. Their style of play is puck possession while playing the game at a top tempo. The basic premise of their style is pressure in all situations. Even when killing a penalty, Russians will attack. They often have a man leave the zone when going out to pressure a puck at the blue line. They like to spread out their players when they have the puck, stretching the defense and creating holes for them to attack the defensive team. They combine good size with small, quick, creative players.

Teams that have success against them play a very simple game. They play physically but smart. Their opponents don't want to spend a lot of time in the penalty box, as the Russians' power-play units are among the best in the world. The opponent must get the puck deep in the Russians' defensive zone and can't afford many turnovers against them. Work them low: They aren't used to playing defense in their own zone.

It's important to get a good start against the Russians. The longer the game goes—whether it's tied or the opponent is in the lead—the better it is for the opponent. The Russians are not used to being in close games or playing from behind. The opponent should shoot on every chance, as Russian goalies don't always match the skill level of their other positions.

It will be interesting to see if their youth hockey developmental system stays intact with so many social changes occurring in the country. Will the youth coaches stay working with the young players or leave for better-paying jobs at higher levels of play?

UNITED STATES

Over the last few years, the United States has experienced some of its greatest accomplishments at the international level (2002 and 2005 under-18 world champions, 2004 and 2013 world junior champions, 2010 Olympic silver medalists). We now compete regularly for medals at all levels of the game. One of the reasons for this recent success is the building of a development program in Ann Arbor, Michigan.

In 1996, USA Hockey provided the funds to create the National Team Development Program. The NTDP draws this country's most talented 16- and 17-year-old hockey players to a centrally located area and lets them train and develop at a high level. With high-quality coaching, scheduling, and training regimens, the program's goal is to develop young U.S. players to secure higher levels of play for international competition. Because of the success of the teams in this program, other countries are researching what we have done to achieve the on-ice success the United States has experienced.

One of the key elements this program provides, besides a solid base of developing the most talented players in the United States, is the fact that when competing in international tournaments, the U.S. team now plays together for more than just two weeks (which was the norm previously). They are a team in the true sense of the word. They know their systems, they know each other, and they have worked through some good times and bad times—they are a team. This provides another truly important aspect when competing at a high level.

When talking to international hockey personnel about the style the Americans play, one comment stands out consistently: Americans play with great vigor. Much like Canada, the United States plays aggressively. The way they forecheck, the emphasis on physical play, and the pace all indicate a high-tempo, high-energy style. The skill level is still not quite as high as some countries around the world, but some wonderfully skilled players are developing, and they play with passion.

Hockey in the United States may not evoke the same level of national pride as found in some other countries, but there are localized areas within the United States that take great pride in playing this game. And although the NTDP is not the perfect model of development, it has been a major factor in the success the United States has enjoyed over the last decade. Like Canada, if the United States continues to push development at a young age and stays away from games and tournaments, the skill level will rise. With the increase in skill and the competitive nature of our athletes, success will be a hallmark of Team USA in future international events.

CONCLUSION

Considering the different styles of hockey mentioned in this chapter, there are several common denominators that bring us together globally. First is the passion that each country has for this game. In some countries, the entire nation lives, breathes, and even measures its national pride, in part, based on how well the national hockey teams perform at the international level. In other countries, there are dedicated pockets that shoulder this same sense of national pride.

Another common denominator is the fact that hockey officials from each country look to improve their nation's level of success by being innovative and analyzing what others are doing well in developing hockey programs. In some cases, reinventing the wheel isn't necessary; simply adopting what others are already doing successfully can be quite efficient. Many countries have schools in which hockey is part of the daily curriculum. Drawing from that notion, USA Hockey created the National Team Development

Program, which brings some of the most talented high school–age hockey players to one location, where they continue school but also train, practice, and play at an accelerated rate. This trend continues to grow, especially in North America.

In reality, the bottom line is we learn from one another through self-analysis and creative approaches to the game. The end result is finding ways to make a wonderful game even better for more young players to enjoy.

About the Editor

Joe Bertagna has been a college hockey administrator for more than 30 years. Since 1997, he has served as commissioner of Hockey East, the preeminent conference in college hockey whose member-schools have earned a combined seven NCAA championships under his leadership. Prior to his move to Hockey East, Bertagna served 15 years with the Eastern College Athletic Conference (ECAC), where he held the positions of tournament director, executive director, and commissioner. Both with ECAC and Hockey East, Bertagna has been a champion of women's hockey, having initiated ECAC Division I and Division III league play and led the formation of the Women's Hockey East Association, whose championship trophy is named in Bertagna's honor.

Courtesy of University of Notre Dame Athletic Media Relations. Photographer: Mike Bennett.

In addition to his commissionership of Hockey East, Bertagna is executive director of the American Hockey Coaches Association, a position he has held since 1991. He also serves on the board of directors of both USA Hockey and the Hockey Humanitarian Award Foundation. Bertagna has for 40 years operated his own clinics for thousands of goalies of all ages throughout New England.

Bertagna began his professional coaching career in 1985 with the National Hockey League's (NHL) Boston Bruins, where he was goaltender coach until 1991, and then again for the 1994-95 season. He also served as goaltender coach for the U.S. Men's National Team at the 1991 Canada Cup, the U.S. Olympic Men's Ice Hockey Team at the 1994 Winter Olympics in Lillehammer, Norway, and the International Hockey League's Milwaukee Admirals from 1994-96.

As a player, Bertagna was a standout collegiate goaltender for Harvard University and, after graduating in 1973, he played professionally for the Milwaukee Admirals and in Cortina, Italy, where the team won the Italian Ice Hockey championship in 1975.

Bertagna and his wife, Kathy, reside in Gloucester, Massachusetts with their three children.

About the Contributors

Tom Anastos, a Michigan State alum, returned to his alma mater in the spring of 2011 to assume the role of head coach. In his four seasons with the team, the Spartans have recorded a 61-75-16 record. Anastos is no stranger to being behind the bench. He served as the head coach at the University of Michigan-Dearborn from 1987-90 and was an assistant under former Michigan State head coach Ron Mason from 1990-92. When not behind the bench, Anastos has  served as the commissioner of the CCHA, president of the Hockey Commissioners Association, and was instrumental in the creation of College Hockey Inc.

Anastos was a standout at Michigan State from 1981-85 and was a part of teams that won three Great Lakes Invitationals, a regular season CCHA Championship, four consecutive CCHA Tournament Titles, and made four NCAA appearances. He skated in 151 games, amassing 143 points on 70 goals and 73 assists. He still holds the single-season short-handed goal recorded with seven back in the 1983-84 season. To cap off his playing career, Anastos spent one year playing in the Montreal Canadiens organization after being drafted by them in the sixth round of the 1981 draft.

Mike Cavanaugh just wrapped up his second season at the helm of the University of Connecticut bench and first season competing in Hockey East. Since taking over the head coaching position, the Huskies have gone 28-33-11. Prior to taking on his current role, Cavanaugh spent 18 seasons at Boston College as an assistant on the staff of legendary coach Jerry York. While at BC, he played an instrumental role in the overall team's success, as well as the individual success of many of his former players.

Cavanaugh spent his playing days at Bowdoin College in Maine. He was a three-year letter winner for the Polar Bears and served as team captain his senior year. He also played on the school's football team, where he was a wide receiver and captain.

Bill Cleary is one of the most successful and decorated individuals to ever pass through amateur hockey in the United States. An All-American hockey player at Harvard University, Cleary still holds the single season scoring record for the Crimson with 89 points. He took his skills into two Olympic Games, earning a silver medal in Cortina d'Ampezzo for coach John Mariucci in 1956 and followed that with a gold medal for coach Jack Riley in Squaw Valley in 1960.

In 1971, he returned to his alma mater as head coach and won over 300 games in a 20-year career, the highlight of which was the 1989 NCAA Championship, Harvard's only NCAA title in hockey. Following his retirement from the bench, Cleary remained at Harvard as director of athletics. His is the only number retired by Harvard in any of its 41 varsity sports.

Rick Comley had a lengthy coaching career, spending 38 years behind the bench for three different teams. A year after graduating from Lake Superior State, he returned to his alma mater as an assistant coach under Ron Mason for the years 1972-73. When Mason departed after that season, Comley took over the helm of the program and stayed there until 1976. After leaving LSSU, he became the head coach at Northern Michigan where he was tasked with starting its varsity program, and he did so successfully. During his time there he won several regular season titles, conference tournament championships, and a National Championship in 1991. In 2002, Comley once again replaced Mason, this time at Michigan State. Here he earned his second National Championship in 2007, becoming only the third coach to ever win the title at two different schools.

Comley spent his playing days at Lake Superior State University from 1967-1971. Over his four years the team compiled a 74-24-6 record. Comley captained the team as a senior and earned team MVP and All-American Honors during his senior season as well. Among his many accolades, he was also honored as LSSU's Most Outstanding Athlete in 1971.

Mark Dennehy completed his tenth season behind the bench of the Merrimack College Warriors in 2015. In the ten seasons that he has been at the helm of the program, the Warriors have gone 128-187-43. Before taking on the head coaching position at Merrimack, he worked under Don Cahoon at Princeton from 1994-99, was the head coach of Fairfield for the 1999-00 season, and then joined Cahoon once again from 2000-05, this time at UMass.

Dennehy played college hockey at perennial Hockey East powerhouse Boston College. During his time as an Eagle, he helped win three Hockey East regular season titles and was a part of the team that won the Hockey East Championship in 1990. After his college career was over, Dennehy went overseas to play for the Ayr Raiders in Britain's elite league during the 1991-92 season.

Mike Eaves returned to his alma mater in 2002 to take over the helm of the Wisconsin hockey team. Since returning to the Badgers, Eaves has coached his teams to a 259-206-35 record, a National Championship in 2006, a WCHA Championship in 2013 and a Big 10 Championship in 2014. Eaves' coaching resume is extensive having had stints in the NHL with Calgary, Philadelphia, and Pittsburgh, in the AHL with Hershey, and overseas in the Finnish Elite

Courtesy of University of Wisconsin Athletic Communications.

League. He has also been the head coach at UW-Eau Claire and at Shattuck St. Mary's High School. Also on his resume are his roles as head coach of the U.S. National Team, U.S. National Junior Team, and the U.S. National Team Development Program.

Eaves was a four-year letter winner for the Badgers from 1974-78. In 160 career games, he posted 267 points on 94 goals and 173 assists and ranks as Wisconsin's all-time scoring leader. During his four seasons he was named a first-team All-American twice and was a part of the 1977 National Championship winning team. After his college career was over, he spent eight years in the NHL playing for Minnesota and Calgary and also represented the U.S. in international play in 1976, 1978, 1981, and 1984.

Guy Gadowsky found himself at the helm of an NCAA Division I program for the 15th time this season. He took on the role of head coach at Penn State in 2011, with the team's inaugural Division I season beginning in 2012. Since 2012, Gadowsky has guided the Nittany Lions to a 39-55-15 record. Prior to Penn State, he served as the head coach of Princeton for seven seasons and before that was the head coach at the University of Alaska for five seasons.

Before joining the ranks of Division I college coaches, Gadowsky served as the head coach and director of hockey operations for the Fresno Falcons of the WCHL from 1996-90.

Gadowsky enjoyed four years of hockey at Colorado College from 1985-1989, before going on to have a seven-year pro career. During his time at Colorado College, he played in 134 games and recorded 46 points. After his college career, he spent time playing in the ECHL, IHL, and AHL, as well as overseas in Austria, the Netherlands, and Sweden.

George Gwozdecky was at the helm of the Denver bench for nineteen seasons from 1994-2013. During his time at Denver, the Pioneers went 443-267-64, won back-to-back National Championships in 2004 and 2005, were crowned WCHA regular season champions three times, and were crowned WCHA Tournament champions four times. Prior to his time spent at Denver, Gwozdecky was the head coach at Wisconsin-River Falls from 1981-84, assistant at  Michigan State from 1984-89, and then head coach at Miami from 1989-94. During his time at Michigan State, he was a part of the 1986 Spartan team that captured the National title. After departing Denver, he joined the Tampa Bay Lightning of the NHL in 2013 as an assistant.

Gwozdecky spent his college days playing at Wisconsin from 1974-78. During his time as a Badger, he saw his team win two regular season titles, a tournament championship, and was a part of the 1978 National Championship winning team. He is the only person to have won a National Championship as a player, assistant coach, and head coach.

Nate Leaman is in his fourth season as the head coach of the Providence College Friars. Since taking over in 2011, the Friars have posted a 77-47-19 record. Prior to taking his current role at Providence College, Leaman spent eight seasons at the helm of the Union men's hockey team from 2003-11. He was the first head coach to leave Union with a winning record after posting a 138-127-35 record in his eight seasons. He also spent time as an assistant  at Harvard from 1999-03. He has since coached Providence College to win the NCAA Men's Ice Hockey Championship in 2015.

Leaman graduated from SUNY Cortland in 1997 where he was a four-year letter winner. He captained the team in both his junior and senior seasons and ranks among the team's top-20 scorers.

The one chapter being published posthumously is that of **E.J. McGuire**. E.J. was born in Buffalo and attended SUNY Brockport where he served as captain of the hockey team and once set a school mark with five assists in a single game. He graduated in 1975, stayed on to get his master's degree, helped the hockey team as an assistant, and eventually became head coach from 1977-1981. His contributions to hockey at Brockport were recognized in 2009 when  he became the first hockey player inducted into the school's Hall of Fame.

Through a chance introduction to Mike Keenan at one of Roger Neilson's coaching clinics in 1980, E.J. embarked on a number of unique coaching experiences alongside the fiery Keenan. They first tasted success in the AHL at Rochester and later with Philadelphia and Chicago of the NHL. Along the way, E.J. found time to get his doctorate in kinesiology, work as head coach of the Maine Mariners in the AHL, at Guelph in the OHL, and assist at the University of Maine during legendary head coach Shawn Walsh's illness. He enjoyed two other assistant stints in the NHL with Ottawa and a second time with Philly before finding a home with Central Scouting in 2002. At the time of his death in 2011, he was NHL Vice-President for Central Scouting.

Marty Palma is in his 12th season as the head coach of the Community College of Allegheny County Division III ice hockey team. He has coached at all levels of youth hockey, including JV and varsity high school. He has served as an instructor at the International Hockey College and holds his coaching certification through USA Hockey. He and his wife, Anne, and daughters Jennifer, Emily, and Katherine reside in Pittsburgh.

Boston University's **Jack Parker** retired from college coaching in 2013, following 40 years and 897 victories, second most in the history of the NCAA and the most wins for any coach at one institution.

Parker was a standout and captain at BU, graduating in the class of 1968. After an apprenticeship serving his alma mater as an assistant, Parker took the reins of the program in 1973 and crafted one of the most successful careers of any coach in college hockey history. Included in those 897 wins were NCAA championships in 1978, 1995, and 2009. He was voted by his peers as national Coach of the Year on two occasions (1978 and 2009), and in 2010, the National Hockey League recognized his contributions to hockey in the United States with the Lester Patrick Award.

Mike Schafer just finished his 20th season behind the bench for Cornell University at the end of the 2014-15 season. Since taking over the helm in 1995, Schafer has lead the program to a 375-222-77 record and ranks as the winningest coach in program history. With his 375 career wins, he ranks among the top-10 active Division I coaches.

Schafer is another coach that returned to his alma mater to coach. While donning the Cornell sweater, Schafer appeared in 107 games, had 70 points on 10 goals and 60 assists, and was a two-year team captain. He was a part of three teams that won a share of the Ivy League crown in consecutive years and as a senior was part of a team that captured the ECAC Championship.

Ben Smith earned a spot in hockey history when he led the United States women's squad to a gold medal in the first Olympic Games that recognized women's ice hockey as a medal sport. The games were held in Nagano, Japan, in 1998. Smith has remained involved with USA Hockey, coaching the U.S. to silver and bronze medals in 2002 and 2006, before becoming a talent evaluator for both the men's and women's national teams.

Prior to his involvement with USA Hockey, Smith coached extensively at the college level, serving as men's head coach at Dartmouth College and Northeastern University, and those positions following stints as an assistant coach at Boston University and Yale. Smith was an outstanding player at Harvard, graduating in 1968.

Hal Tearse's playing career ended his sophomore year at the University of Minnesota. He began coaching that same year and retired from coaching following the 2013-14 season at Providence Academy. Hal continues to serve as the program coordinator and part time assistant coach at the school as well as an assistant coach on AA Bantam team in the Twin Cities. He also continues to serve Minnesota Hockey as safety director and focuses on reducing injuries through fair play and by increasing player skills at all levels.

He and his wife, Lynn, and son, David, recently moved to Independence, Minnesota from Plymouth, and his daughter, Nicole, lives in Minneapolis.

Michael Zucker has been coaching hockey since 1997 with stints at the NCAA Division I (NCHC), Tier 1 Junior A (USHL), and Canadian Major Junior (WHL) levels. Having learned from some of the best coaches in the business, including former NHL head coach, Kevin Constantine, current NHL assistant coach, George Gwozdecky, and the winningest coach in the history of USA Junior Hockey, Bliss Littler, he co-founded Bench Metrics LLC, a hockey analytics software company. In the past ten seasons, Michael has coached 39 NHL draft picks, six of whom were selected in the first round of the NHL entry draft. A native of Queens, New York, Michael now resides in Seattle, Washington.

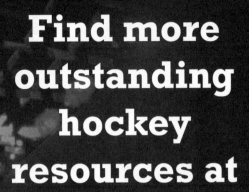